Bread Machine Cook

1200 Days of Easy and Tasty Recipes for Beginners to Fully Enjoy Your Bread Machine and Give Your Fresh, Delicious Homemade Bread an Extra Touch

OLIVIA MARINI

Contents

Introduction

The recipes for bread made in the bread machine are outstanding. They are the easiest and most easy way to create bread that is both nutritious and tasty without having to put in a lot of work. You should read this book if you are interested in learning more about the science that lies behind these recipes so that you may choose the one that suits your tastes the best. In an effort to get you in the kitchen, we have gathered together some of the best recipes that we could discover on the internet. Kindly describe what a bread maker is in more detail. In the comfort of one's own home, one may use a bread machine to bake loaves of bread. Typically, it consists of an electric motor that is coupled to a paddle that mixes and kneads the dough, and it has a variety of settings for making various types of loaves, such as white, whole wheat, rye, and French bread. Some versions even have as many as twelve separate presets that may be used to bake a variety of foods, such as cakes, doughnuts, pizzas, and other items. A bread machine is an excellent item to have if you want to be self-sufficient in baking but don't have much time to make it yourself. If this describes you, read on. Because the whole process of mixing, kneading, and rising is automated, this approach is fantastic for those who have busy schedules but still want to enjoy the benefits of freshly baked bread. The wonderful scent that fills the whole household while fresh bread is baking is hard to beat.

For those who have never baked before, using a bread machine to make bread is an excellent way to get started in the hobby. Because the machines perform all the work, anybody can make a wonderful loaf of bread without having to worry about whether or not the dough has properly risen, fermented, or cooked itself. This is because the machines do all the work. People who want to bake bread but don't have the time to devote to the process for a whole day will find this extremely useful. To utilize a bread machine from beginning to finish requires no more than three to four hours of your time. People who are allergic to gluten have the option of using the bread machine's pre-set programs to produce wheat-free bread that tastes deliciously sweet despite not containing any wheat. Certain versions are equipped with dough attachments that let the user to create pasta, pizza, and biscuits. If you want to use bread as the base for other meals, such as pies, tarts, or quiches, you can consider purchasing a bread machine that also includes attachments for manufacturing doughnuts, cakes, or other types of pastries. You are free to experiment with alternative recipes and modify the proportions so that they are more to your taste given that these basic models are comprised of configurable factors. There are several bread machines that will set you back a fair coin. When you consider the amount of time and effort you save by not having to shop for ingredients and knead the dough by hand, using a bread machine is not nearly as expensive as you may think it would be since you get an extra loaf of bread out of the deal. Even a very little initial investment will result in a return in a matter of weeks or months. Even if you don't have the time or energy to make your own bread, you could enjoy the smell of freshly made loaves nevertheless.

This book is designed for 1200 days, as you can enjoy mixing and replicating the recipes presented with all your imagination for well beyond the next thousand days!

Chapter 1: Bread Machine And Baking

A bread machine or bread maker is an absolute blessing for those who have never attempted to bake bread before but are nonetheless interested in giving it a go. They are able to bake like professionals with dependably delicious outcomes in terms of both the texture and flavor of the bread since the bread dough is made in a bread machine. It is equipped with self-sufficient procedures that enable it to mix, knead, and form the dough without the assistance of a person. Because it is an electronic device, it allows you to bake bread in the length of time and at the temperature that you choose, regardless of how long it takes. Because bread is a necessity in the majority of households and because it is difficult to imagine formulating a meal plan that does not contain bread, owning a bread machine may be of great assistance. There is always a bread pan on the interior of the bread machine to contain the dough, and there are always paddles connected to the bottom of the pan. The heating element of the machine is permanently positioned within it, which enables it to provide warmth that is consistent throughout the chamber.

To put it another way, one may use a bread machine to produce a delicious loaf of bread. Because it is so simple to bake your own bread with the assistance of a bread machine, this appliance is an invaluable addition to any kitchen. It just takes a few minutes to load the machine with the ingredients, and it consistently makes bread that is cooked to perfection in the loaf pans. Many types of bread, including white bread, whole wheat bread, rye bread, and even sweet treats like doughnuts and cakes, may be produced in the many beadmakers that are available for purchase in stores and on the internet. It is highly recommended that you go with a model that comes equipped with a paddle that can be used to move the dough about the baking pan while it is cooking. Breads may differ from one another in terms of texture, flavor, and appearance depending on the components that go into making them. In contrast to a standard oven, a bread machine requires a particular set of baking instructions to be programmed into it before it can begin the process of baking dough. If you are required to consume a gluten-free diet, search for a bread maker that can completely remove gluten from their loaves or reduce the quantity of gluten present by a significant amount. If you are new to baking and are unsure how to get started, you should look for a model that has buttons that are specifically designated for particular activities. If you have a lot of experience baking, it is recommended that you choose a model that gives you a lot of different options and settings to play around with. The quality of the ingredients that are used in a bread machine is comparable to the quality of the ingredients that are used in real bread. Because there is such a vast range of breads that may be baked, it is essential to utilize high-quality flour. The quality and flavor of the bread that is produced by a bread machine are mostly determined by the parameters that are selected by the user. Make sure you use the right amount of flour and water for your preferred loaf recipe. Keep track of the time for the dough cycle and decide how long you want the dough to rest once it has been risen. Do not assume that you will get the same results even if you alter the settings simply because you always use the same sort of dough even if you have done so in the past. When compared to white bread, the rising time for bread made with whole wheat or rye flour is much lower due to the reduced amount of gluten that is needed. Using a bread machine to make dough for homemade pizza is a simple process. My go-to, to which you can add any kind of precooked meat or vegetables as well as pretty much anything else you would want. If you want to make something delicious, but not cookies or cakes, an ice cream maker could be a beneficial item for you to utilize. With addition to bread, biscuits may be baked in a bread machine. When planning your next cooking or baking endeavor, it is a good idea to stock up on a selection of dry milk, eggs, sweeteners, and spices like instant coffee. Some bread makers even come with their own accessories and recipes already saved inside the machine itself, however this varies from model to model. A bread machine makes it easy to create excellent white or wheat loaves, regardless of whether you are an experienced baker or not. This is true regardless of whether you have ever baked before or not. Utilizing this convenient small appliance, you can provide your family with freshly baked bread and snacks.

Chapter 2: Getting Started With Your Bread Machine

Experiment with delayed baking, different types of cycle, and loaves of differing lengths to get a feel for the bread machine's functionality and the breadth of customization possibilities it offers. It's possible that you'll need to experiment with a few different recipes and components before you find the ideal combination. In order to fulfill this function, several devices come with blank or pre-filled setup cards already stored in memory. You may save a bread recipe on one of these cards, along with instructions or a note to remind you of the criteria that resulted in the greatest bread, if you want to do so. Getting all of the parts in working order Choose the kind of bread that you would want to prepare. In the event that you are unclear as to the amount of flour or any of the other components, you should reference the recipe book or the manual.

You may avoid manually measuring the flour or liquids by using the measurement container that is already included into the machine. Prepare the bread pan in accordance with the instructions provided by the manufacturer. Prepare the automatic bread maker. Check the owner's manual to learn more about the different cycles that come with your machine. It's possible that the kind of bread you want to make will also have an impact on the timetable you go with. You can program a computer to do anything. You will need to read the manual for your particular computer if you want to learn how to do this task on it. The device's capability to function may be delayed until a certain time of day rather than being activated instantly. Be sure to verify the machine's software thoroughly and re-program it if required if the issue is not resolved. After the bread pan has been placed into the bread machine, the ingredients may be poured in. There are bread machines on the market that may be purchased with either a removable or non-removable pan. Place all of the ingredients in the pan in the order that corresponds to their addition.

Give it some time. Put the machine into operation. If you take the time to prepare the machine for operation before going to bed, you should find that your sleep is more rejuvenating in the morning. You may use the timer feature on certain appliances to start the baking process at a later time if you are aware that you will be absent when the bread is first removed from the oven. Check the bread after it has been toasted. Remove the bread from the machine when the cycle has finished, and if it is ready, do it while wearing oven gloves to protect your fingertips from the heat generated by the lid. After it has fully cooled, remove it off the wire rack and cut it into pieces that are appropriate for serving.

Chapter 3: Benefits And Disadvantages Of A Bread Machine

When we could merely bake the bread in the oven, it doesn't seem essential to use a bread machine. That is a very reasonable question to ask. Breads Just Baked A bread machine will generate dough that is instantly ready to go into the oven once it has been used. The dough should remain within the machine until it is time to utilize it. It is possible that it will keep the dough at room temperature in the meanwhile. If you use a bread machine, you won't need to remove dough from the refrigerator many hours in advance of when you want to serve it. Control must be exercised over the components. If you bake bread by hand, it's easy to use too much or too little of an ingredient. However, if you use a bread machine, you can be certain to use the exact proper quantity of each ingredient and you can fine-tune the bread's texture to your taste.

No Clutter It is not the labor required to generate perfect dough that constitutes the main work at hand; rather, it is the mess that must be produced once the dough has been made. The amount of time spent cleaning up that mess is going to be more than the amount of time spent actually producing the dough. The usage of a bread machine, on the other hand, renders this problem irrelevant since the raw ingredients are meticulously combined into a smooth dough while still within the machine itself. There is a possibility that both your working surface and the mixing tool will stay clutter-free. Money-Saving Because it will aid with every step of the process, purchasing a bread machine will remove the need for any other electrical equipment in the kitchen. This is because it will help with baking bread. In addition to this, it makes delicious bread in a very short length of time while using a little amount of electricity.

This Is Much More Than a Normal Bread Machine! This bread machine can handle a variety of batters and doughs in addition to bread dough, so its usage is not restricted to the production of just bread dough. With the assistance of this enchanted appliance in the kitchen, you are able to prepare a wide range of foods. The two steps in the process of making bread that take the most time and are considered to be the most important — kneading and leavening — can now be accomplished with ease and precision in a bread machine, which ensures that the bread will always have an outstanding texture and flavor. If you want to ensure that the bread is of a high quality and bake like a pro, you could find that using a bread machine is useful.

Disadvantages

- It's tougher to bake intricate loaves (i.e., glazed breads).
- It takes more effort to bake different shaped loaves of bread (i.e., long baguettes).
- The outlay of funds needed to purchase a bread maker.
- Homemade bread often goes stale more rapidly than store-bought bread (because store breads often contain chemical preservatives).
- Inability to bake bread in sufficiently enough quantities. Most bread machines have a maximum loaf weight setting of two pounds.
- Most bread machine loaves have a "hole" in the bottom where the mixing paddle fits.
- Using a bread machine may occasionally generate "confusion" when following a recipe due to the wide variety of bread makers available. Examples include bread machines with settings that seem similar but are really used for different kinds of baking (such speedy and quick bread), leading to customer confusion.
- Simpler bread machines often have fewer settings for personalizing the baked goods.

Chapter 4: How Do You Store Bread

If you're like most people, you probably don't have a lot of time to spend on bread storage. That's why it's important to find a guide that can help you store bread efficiently and effectively. There are many different ways to store bread, so it's important to find a guide that can provide the best instruction for your needs. This guide will provide an overview of how to store bread, as well as tips on how to make the most of your storage space.

Bread is a type of food that is meant to be eaten fresh or frozen. It is made from flour, water, and salt. Bread is usually served as a snack or in a sandwich.

Bread can be stored in many ways, but the most common way to store bread is by placing it in an airtight container. The best way to store bread is to keep it cool and protected from bacteria and other pests. Freezable bread should also be stored in an airtight container for at least 3 months.

To make bread, you will need flour, water, and salt. In order to mix these ingredients together, you will need a bowl or measuring cup. Next, you will need to add oil or butter to the bowl or measuring cup so that the mixture can start Mixing properly

Next, you will need to add enough of the dough ingredients until it forms a ball

Once the dough has formed a ball, you can place it in an oiled bowl or plastic bag

Once the dough has been placed in an oiled bowl or plastic bag, you can put it back into the refrigerator for 30-40 minutes

After the 30-40 minutes have passed, you can take the dough out of the fridge and let it rise for about 20-25 minutes

After the dough has risen, you can shape it into a ball and place it back in the refrigerator

Once the dough has been shaped into a ball, you can place it back in an oiled bowl or plastic bag

How to Store Bread.

Bread should be preheated before storage in order to ensure that it does not spoil. Place bread on a baking sheet and bake at 350 degrees Fahrenheit for about 30 minutes, or until golden brown.

Keep the bread in the fridge, if possible, as it will last up to two days without spoiling. If you have to store the bread in an open space, such as a pantry or living room, make sure to place it in a dry place with minimal moisture so that the bread does not rot.

Tips for Making Bread.

The first step in making bread is to preheat the oven. This will help get the dough nice and warm before shaping it into loafs or rolls.

Place the dough on a baking sheet

Bread dough needs to be placed on a baking sheet in order to bake evenly. Be sure that the dough is well-coated with flour so that it doesn't stick to your hand or pan.

Keep the dough in the fridge

If you want to keep your bread fresh, you should place it in the fridge before baking it. This will help stop the fermentation process from happening and make your bread softer and more pleasant to eat.

Bread is a type of bread that is popular in many countries. It is made from flour and water, and it is an important part of the diet. You can store bread in various ways, depending on how often you will need it. It's important to preheat the oven when making bread so that it doesn't get too warm or dry, and to keep the dough in the fridge if you plan on using it soon. By following these tips, you can make delicious and nutritious bread every time.

Chapter 5: Tips And Tricks

You'll discover a lot of useful suggestions in this area, whether you're baking bread for the first time or simply want to make better treats in general. Everything from the bare essentials to simple fixes is right here at your fingertips. Add salt to taste! Salt is an essential component of the recipe, and if you try to exclude it, you will be required to make specific adjustments to the sodium-based formula (in which case, you can buy a reduced or no-sodium version). In addition to that, the recipe could be scrapped if it seems that there won't be any adjustments made. Make the investment in a conversion app, chart, or magnet for the refrigerator. Additionally, you may find it helpful to have conversion manuals on hand for the kitchen. You will have total faith in your capabilities, which will serve you well whether you need to make a switch or modify the measurements.

When you always have a set of conversions and alternatives on hand, it will make all of your baking and culinary endeavors much more fun. If you discover that you are always in the early phases of a process, just before you get the hang of things, it is in your best interest to play it safe and adhere to the guidelines as precisely as you can. You shouldn't worry about following these guidelines until you've had some experience in the real world. When it comes to baking, the delectability is in the details, and you simply cannot afford to make basic errors with the proportions. There is a purpose for the recipe, and if you want excellent results, you should follow the procedures precisely as they are stated. If you want to get good results, follow the recipe. Maintaining Strict Adherence to High Quality Standards It is essential to make use of materials that are consistent with one another.

That's not to suggest that flour sold under a store's own brand couldn't be just as good as flour sold under a more well-known brand; it most definitely can. Nevertheless, paying close attention to choosing components of a good quality is essential to achieving success. Visit a bakery supply or a local bakery if you have the opportunity to do so, so that you may stock up on the delicious foods at a reduced price. You should educate yourself if you do not know what fundamental components you require or which ones are the most effective. If you are familiar with your own baking abilities and preferences, it will be easier for you to home in on the areas in which dependability is most crucial. Please keep these helpful hints in mind in preparation. Even when you're making bread, you shouldn't overlook the importance of taking into consideration the higher protein quality counts that your flour has. Greater quantities of protein result in gluten that is more resilient, which in turn produces superior bread. Cake flour is perfect for use in the production of cakes and other sweets because it has a finer texture than regular flour and fewer proteins than regular flour. All Recipes Serve a Purpose The majority of chefs choose to "throw in" the ingredients or rapidly weigh them, which is OK if you are an experienced chef or if you are creating a meal that you have prepared a hundred times before. However, if you want to make it again from a cookbook, you will need to make certain adjustments to the recipe. Even if you make a little mistake like forgetting an ingredient or overestimating how much of it you need, the final product of your bread might still turn out quite differently. If you want to avoid carelessly messing things up, baking probably isn't the best hobby for you.

However, if you've never used a bread machine before, you could get the feel of things by practicing a few times with the recipe in your hand and the baking temperature in your head. This is especially helpful for those who are just starting out. Even if you have gotten into the routine of creating your own recipes, it is still a good idea to write down at least a rough estimate of how much of each ingredient you will need. It is difficult to add recipes that do not have accurate quantities because of this. The majority of individuals are unable to correctly measure what "a little" of anything is, yet you most likely are aware of the exact quantity that constitutes a "little" of salt. Baking is a process that, due to the fact that it, like cooking, requires knowledge, and so need to be valued in the same manner. Stop: Check That Your Preferences Are Correct Even in this case, the mechanism is quite important. It is recommended that you verify the settings of your bread machine before beginning to use a new baking program. This will allow you to get the most out of your bread machine. You should always do a second check, even if you believe that you have left it on the correct setting or that you have supplied the correct function. Losing an hour of time due to a wrong setting is one of the most aggravating things that may happen.

It seems that your recipe was a complete failure at this point. The default configurations should be sufficient for the vast majority of first-time users. People who have previous knowledge with kitchen machines such as bread makers have access to a few more possibilities, and in the end, everyone will be able to get at their destination. Utilize the capabilities provided by the computer if you are unsure how to proceed with an essential choice. You will have outstanding results, and even if the program is not flawless, you will have something to improve on. This is an extremely rare combination. Buttermilk Fundamentals There is a chance that some of the people who read this are not acquainted with buttermilk. The great majority of bakers are completely clueless about the purpose of this odd component. It is not necessary for you to feel guilty about this. Buttermilk was the name given to the liquid that remained after sugar had been churned out of cream after the process.

Every single bottle of buttermilk that is offered in supermarkets today has been either grown or modified from its original form in some way. The use of buttermilk helps to accentuate the delicate tang that is already present in baked products. Through a reaction with the baking soda called for in the recipe, it causes breads and baked goods to rise more effectively. There are several recipes for baked goods that call for buttermilk. On the other hand, not everyone has a supply of buttermilk laying around. There is a workaround for situations in which you do not routinely have it on hand or in which you are preparing a baking job at the eleventh hour. You will be required to bring a cup that is suitable for measuring liquids (one cup is fine). The measuring cup should now have the juice of a half of a lemon in it. After that, fill the milk container up to the mark that indicates the halfway point. If you let it rest for some time, you'll end up with buttermilk that you can use right away in the kitchen. Put the Past in the Past and Focus on the Present and Future It is advised that you try new things. If you are just beginning to make bread or use a bread machine, you shouldn't depart too much from the conventional techniques that are typically followed. In any event, if you are prepared to run the risk of being unsuccessful in order to make progress, you should try out as many different things as possible.

As you gain experience using your bread machine, you will get the confidence to make adjustments to various aspects of the process and learn more about what you are capable of doing on your own. As one instance, applesauce is often used in the place of sugar in the preparation of baked products. Experimenting with various spices, baking periods, temperatures, and even your bread machine may help you get the best possible outcomes in your baking endeavors. Examens de la continuity When baking bread, consistency is the single most crucial component, so be sure to keep a close check on it just like you would with any other technique of cooking. Despite the fact that the age-old "lightly brown" criterion is still usually valid, the quality of the finished product may vary quite a bit when utilizing baking equipment such as a bread machine.

Make advantage of the "pause" option on your oven and check on your baked goods at regular intervals to guarantee that they will turn out flawlessly. Your baking plan shouldn't see too much of a disruption as a result of this. It is presumed that a single example is enough. When baking bread, it is a good idea to take frequent pauses in order to check on the development of the bread and to remove the paddle. It not only allows you to extract the paddle before it becomes cooked into the bread and impossible to remove, but it also enables you to guarantee that correct measurements are taken.

Chapter 6: Basic Bread Recipes

Loaf With Bacon, Tomatoes, And Cheddar Cheese.

Cooking Time: 40 Minutes
Servings: 2
Nutritional Analysis:

Calories: 170

Total Fat: 3.25 g

Carbohydrates: 30 g

Fiber: 1.0 g

Ingredients:

- 4 cups of cold water
- Amount: 4 tablespoons of dried active yeast 1 tablespoon of sugar
- Bread flour, at least 3 cups (2 ounces) and more if required
- Ingredients: 2 cups (3 ounces) semolina flour
- chopped sun-dried tomatoes equivalent to ounces
- 1 pound of bacon, cooked 6 ounces of Cheddar, diced
- (I set aside one tablespoon of grease)
- chopped, crushed, or otherwise shredded Nonstick baking spray 2 teaspoons of kosher salt

Instructions:

- Blend everything together and knead it until it's elastic, either by hand (mix in a big basin, then turn out and knead) or in a stand mixer with a dough hook. The dough itself should be elastic, but the texture will be lumpy.
- The dough needs approximately an hour to rise to double its original size, so cover the bowl and set it in a warm place.
- In the meanwhile, prepare a 9x5-inch loaf pan by spraying it with cooking spray.
- Place the dough on a floured surface and shape it into a rough 8-inch square. Roll the top half down to meet the centre, then press the edge down to seal. Refold the top, getting as close as possible (within an inch)
- Therefore, from the ground up. Seal the edge by pressing down. Now, close the seam by grabbing the dough's base and pulling it up to meet the roll. Seal the ends with a pinch and lay the dough in the pan, seam side down.
- Wrap the pan with plastic wrap or set it inside a big plastic bag, then secure the bag's open end. Put the dough in the fridge for at least 12 hours and up to 24 hours before you want to bake it. A longer rest is beneficial to the dough, but it should be completely risen after around 6 hours.
- Remove the dish from the fridge, and set the oven temperature to 350 degrees Fahrenheit. One rack should be positioned in the exact middle of the oven.
- Take the bread out of the bag and bake it for another 10-15 minutes, or until an instant-read thermometer inserted into the center registers 195 degrees Fahrenheit.
- Time taken: 55 minutes. When the bread is done baking, remove it from the pan and let it cool on a wire rack.

Toasted Loaf Of Oatmeal, Honey, And Dates

Cooking Time: 30 Minutes
Servings: 2
Nutritional Analysis:

Calories: 160

Total Fat: 3.0g

Carbohydrates: 28 g

Fiber: 2g

Ingredients:

- The equivalent of one cup of rolled oats
- White rye flour, 2 cups (about 8 ounces)
- Bread flour, at least 2 cups (14 ounces) and up to as much as
- honey, tablespoons
- 4 cups of water, at room temperature
- Half a teaspoon of table salt 1 ounce of olive oil
- Four Tablespoons of Dry Yeast That Is Already Active
- dates, about 2 cups worth, chopped Oil-free cooking spray

Instructions:

- Blend everything together and knead it until it's elastic, either by hand (mix in a big basin, then turn out and knead) or in a stand mixer with a dough hook. The dough itself should be elastic, but the texture will be lumpy.
- The dough needs approximately an hour to rise to double its original size, so cover the bowl and set it in a warm place.
- In the meanwhile, prepare a 9x5-inch loaf pan by spraying it with cooking spray.
- Place the dough on a floured surface and shape it into a rough 8-inch square. Roll the top half down to meet the centre, then press the edge down to seal. The top should be folded over once again, this time until it's within a half an inch of the bottom. Seal the edge by pressing down. Now, pinch the bottom of the dough and roll it up to meet the rest of the dough, sealing the two together. Seal the ends with a pinch and lay the dough in the pan, seam side down.
- Wrap the pan with plastic wrap or set it inside a big plastic bag, then secure the bag's open end. Put in the fridge at least 12 hours, and up to 24, before using. A longer rest is beneficial to the dough, but it should be completely risen after around 6 hours.
- Remove the dish from the fridge, and set the oven temperature to 350 degrees Fahrenheit.
- After 55 minutes, take the bread out of the oven and remove the plastic wrap. Continue baking until a thermometer inserted into the center registers 195 degrees Fahrenheit. Take the bread out of the pan and let it cool on a rack before cutting into it.

Product Made With Almond Flour

Cooking Time: 30 Minutes
Servings: 3
Nutritional Analysis:

Calories: 180

Total Fat: 3g

Carbohydrates: 25g

Fiber: 2 g

Ingredients:

- A total of 4 egg whites
- Two whole eggs
- 2 cups of ground almonds 14 cup melted butter
- Psyllium husk powder, 2 teaspoons one and a half teaspoons of baking powder Xanthan gum, half a teaspoon
- Salt
- Half a cup plus two teaspoons of hot water 2-and-a-quarter teaspoons of yeast

Instructions:

- Combine everything in a small mixing basin except the yeast.
- The wet ingredients should be placed in the bread machine's pan.
- Put all the dry ingredients, which have been accumulated in the bottom bowl, into the pan of the bread machine. Sprinkle the yeast over the top.
- Using the bread setting, program the bread maker to make standard bread.
- Once the bread is done baking, take the pan out of the bread machine.
- Reserve on a cooling rack after a brief resting period.
- You may keep the bread for up to four days in the fridge, or you can freeze it for up to three months.

Flour From Coconut Meat

Cooking Time: 40 Minutes
Servings: 2
Nutritional Analysis:

Calories: 160

Total Fat: 2 g

Carbohydrates: 28 g

Fiber: 1g

Ingredients:

- 6 eggs
- Just under a cup's worth of coconut flour
- Psyllium husk, 2 teaspoons

- 1/4 cup of olive oil
- 1.25 grams of salt
- Xanthan gum, one tablespoon's worth

Instructions:

- One Tablespoon of Baking Powder 2-and-a-quarter teaspoons of yeast
- Except for the yeast, mix all of the dry ingredients in a small mixing basin.
- The wet ingredients should be placed in the bread machine's pan.
- Dump the contents of the small bowl into the pan of the bread maker. Sprinkle the yeast over the top.
- Using the bread setting, program the bread maker to make standard bread.
- Taking out the baking pan from a bread machine is the last step before removing the finished loaf.
- Transfer to a cooling rack after a little rest.
- Stocking up on bread is a good idea since it keeps for up to four days in the fridge and three months in the freezer.

The Cloud's Savory Bread Loaf

Cooking Time: 30 Minutes
Servings: 1
Nutritional Analysis:

Calories: 190

Total Fat: 3g

Carbohydrates: 25g

Fiber: 1g

Ingredients:

- Whites from 6 eggs
- A total of 6 egg yolks
- Unflavored whey protein powder, 1/2 cup 1/2 teaspoon of cream of tartar
- Sour cream, 6 ounces

Instructions:

- Baking powder, half a teaspoon's Garlic powder, one-fourth teaspoon Garlic powder; 1/2 teaspoon; onion powder; Salinity: One-Fourth Teaspoon
- Egg whites with cream of tartar added should be beaten until firm peaks form. Putting aside.
- Toss the remaining ingredients together in a separate dish.
- Slowly combine the two mixes by folding them together.
- Put the ingredients in the pan of your bread maker.
- In order to make rapid bread, program the bread maker accordingly.
- The bread is done when the pan is taken out of the bread maker.
- Let cool for a while, then place in a cooling bracket.
- Bread may be stored for up to 3 days if kept in an airtight container.

Bread For Sandwiches

Cooking Time: 45 Minutes
Servings: 2
Nutritional Analysis:

Calories: 190

Total Fat: 4 g

Carbohydrates: 20g

Fiber: 3g

Ingredients:

- 4 eggs
- Almond meal, 2 and a half ounces
- 1 tbsp. coconut flour 1 oz. psyllium
- 1 1/2 cups shredded eggplant with the liquids drained Sesame seeds, about 3 teaspoons
- One and a Half Teaspoons of Baking Powder Adequate salting
- Scramble the eggs, and then fold in the grated eggplant.

Instructions:

- Combine the dry ingredients in a separate bowl.
- Combine them with the eggs. Combine in a harmonious manner.
- Place the buns, hand-formed, on a baking sheet lined with parchment paper.
- Cook for 20-25 minutes at 374 degrees Fahrenheit.

The Bread Of France

Cooking Time: 30 Minutes
Servings: 2
Nutritional Analysis:

Calories: 165

Total Fat: 5g

Carbohydrates: 25g

Fiber: 2g

Ingredients:

- 13 cup of hot water Half a Tablespoon of Olive Oil Ample saltiness, or 1 1/2 teaspoons
- teaspoons of salt
- 2 tablespoons active dry yeast 4 cups all-purpose flour
- If you have a bread machine, start by filling it with warm water.

Instructions:

- Lastly, add the olive oil, followed by the salt and then the sugar. Take care to stick to that specific sequence. After that, add the flour. Be careful to conceal the liquids.
- Create a shallow well in the middle of the flour. The indentation must not reach the liquid's surface. The yeast should be inserted into the crater.
- Prepare French bread in the bread maker by selecting the French Bread Cycle.
- Check on the dough after it has been kneaded for 5 minutes. If the dough is too dry and stiff, add a half a tablespoon of water at a time until it can be rolled into a soft ball.
- One tablespoon of flour may be added if the dough is too wet, and so on, until the desired consistency is attained. Wait 10 minutes for the bread to cool before slicing.

Ground-Up Hazelnut And Honey Bread

Cooking Time: 30 Minutes
Servings: 1
Nutritional Analysis:

Calories: 153

Total Fat: 3.2g

Carbohydrates: 28.9g

Fiber: 1.3g

Ingredients:

- 12 cup of room temperature milk
- 1 stick of melted, cooled butter (2 teaspoons) 2 tsp of honey in liquid form
- 1/3 of a teaspoon of salt
- A third of a cup of wild rice, cooked and cooled Two-thirds of a cup of all-purpose flour
- Half a teaspoon of dill weed Sifted almond flour to equal 1 cup
- 1 tsp. of dried active yeast A quarter of a cup of chopped hazelnuts
- Gather your bread's ingredients and measurement tools (a cup, a spoon, kitchen scales).
- Don't forget the nuts and seeds as you carefully measure the rest of the ingredients into the pan.

Instructions:

- Put everything in the bread bucket, but be sure to do it in the appropriate sequence!
- Then use your bread maker as directed in the included instructions.
- Put the lid back on.
- Start your bread machine, and choose the basic setting with a medium crust.
- To begin, please press the start button.
- When the timer goes off, mix in the seeds and nuts.
- Until the program finishes, please be patient. Once it's done, remove the bucket and let it aside for 5-10 minutes to cool off.
- After 30 minutes on the cooling rack, give the loaf a good shake to remove it from the pan.
- Aromatic handmade bread, sliced and ready to be devoured.

Bacon And Eggs

Cooking Time: 30 Minutes
Servings: 2
Nutritional Analysis:

Calories: 183

Total Fat: 4.28 g

Carbohydrates: 26.89 g

Fiber: 1.5 g

Ingredients:

- Four and a half cups of almond flour, plus one cup of milk
- 2 eggs
- 1.25 grams salt 1.25 grams yeast
- a quarter-cup of sugar and a half-cup of butter
- Set up the ingredients in the bread pan as directed by the manufacturer. As a first step, we'll pour in some warm milk and season it with salt.
- Then, add the eggs (which you should first loosen with a fork) and the butter, which you should add after it has melted and cooled to a warm temperature.

Instructions:

- Almond flour, after being sifted, should now be added.
- Dry active yeast should be used for the top as it does not need to be rehydrated.
- Yeast and sugar should be combined at the very end.
- Pick the bare-bones software option (on mine, it is 1 of 12). A timer will count down from 3 hours. The most important part of the process occurs at the start of the batch. In this setup, kneading takes exactly 10 minutes.
- when everything is rolled up into one big sphere.
- After the first four to five minutes of kneading, it should have formed sufficiently for you to assist the bread machine. At first, you should remove the flour that has accumulated on the sides of the bowl because the blade has not been able to fully grab it. Second, it's important to check the flour carefully since various brands use varying amounts of moisture, so you may need to add a little extra, on the order of two to three tablespoons. When the dough is too loose to form a ball.
- Occasionally, but not often enough, not enough liquid causes the dough to become lumpy. If that's the case, you may assist the bread machine knead the dough by adding a little extra water.
- When the signal sounds, in precisely three hours, the house will be filled with the wonderful smell of freshly baked bread. Stop the machine, lift the cover, and remove the bread. Handsome! If the paddle sinks to the bottom of the hot egg bread loaf, take it out of the bowl. Lay the bread on a grate to cool as it cools. Bread is best cooled on its side for maximum efficiency.
- The height of this loaf, at 12 centimeters, is unusually high.
- Once the bread has cooled fully, you may slice it.
- Do everything you can!

Pure White Bread

Cooking Time: 40 Minutes
Servings: 3
Nutritional Analysis:

Calories: 192

Total Fat: 4g

Carbohydrates: 27.79 g

Fiber: 1g

Ingredients:

- Approximately 110 degrees Fahrenheit (45 degrees Celsius) of water (1 cup) is considered lukewarm. White sugar, 3 tablespoons
- 1/2 a teaspoon of salt
- Three Tablespoons of Oil, Veggie Add 3 cups of bread flour
- Active dry yeast, 2 and 1/4 tablespoons

Instructions:

- Add the following to the bread machine: water, sugar, salt, oil, bread flour, and yeast.
- White Bread, Baked According to Instructions. You should let it cool on wire racks before cutting it.

Dough For Ciabatta

Cooking Time: 30 Minutes
Servings: 3
Nutritional Analysis:

Calories: 183

Total Fat: 3.2g

Carbohydrates: 28 g

Fiber: 1 g

Ingredients:

- 1.5 ounces of water
- 1.5 grams of salt
- Exactly one white sugar teaspoon 2 teaspoons butter 3 and a quarter cups of bread flour
- Yeast for bread machine: 1 1/2 teaspoon
- Except for the olive oil, combine all of the ingredients in a stand mixer. On low speed, use a dough hook to combine. Keep mixing for ten minutes. If necessary, scrape the sides.
- After 5 minutes, add the olive oil and continue whisking.
- Stickiness and wetness in the dough are desirable qualities; they will keep you from wanting to add additional flour.
- Place the dough in a large basin or on a sheet of greased plastic wrap and let it rest for 15 minutes.
- Flour baking sheets lightly or use parchment paper.

Instructions:

- Using a sharp knife, cut the dough in half lengthwise, and roll out each half into an oval about 3 by 14 inches.
- Spread the loaves out on floured sheets.
- Wrap the dough into loaves and let them rise in a warm, draft-free place for 45 minutes.
- Turn the oven temperature up to 425 degrees Fahrenheit. Spray water on the bread.
- Put the loaves on the center rack of the oven.
- Bake for 25 to 35 minutes, or until a deep golden brown.
- Have fun as you serve.

Very Simple Bread For The Bread Machine

Cooking Time: 40 Minutes
Servings: 3
Nutritional Analysis:

Calories: 153

Total Fat: 3.9g

Carbohydrates: 25.9 g

Fiber: 1g

Ingredients:

- 227 grams (1 cup) of room temperature water 1/3 cup of heated milk (74 g) Amount: 3 tablespoons (around 43 grams) butter
- Three and a half cups (447 g) of unbleached all-purpose flour Use 35 grams of sugar, which is around 3 teaspoons.
- 1.25 grams of salt
- To activate dried yeast or quick yeast: 1 1/2 teaspoons

Instructions:

- You must put the ingredients in your machine in the sequence recommended by the maker.
- Put some instructions into the bread maker's plain white display and push the start button.
- When a loaf is done baking, take it out of the oven. After 5 minutes, give the pan a little shake to loosen the loaf before turning it out onto a cooling rack.
- Keep for four days if wrapped properly or freeze for up to three months.

The Olive Oil Bread Machine

Cooking Time: 40 Minutes
Servings: 3
Nutritional Analysis:

Calories: 153

Total Fat: 3.9g

Carbohydrates: 25.9 g

Fiber: 1g

Ingredients:

- steaming mug of liquid
- white sugar by the cupful
- Use just 1.25 grams of yeast for the bread machine. A quarter cup of olive oil
- Bread flour equivalent to two and a half cups
- 1/4 cup all-purpose flour Use about a half a spoonful of salt.

Instructions:

- Fill the basin of your bread maker with water, sugar, and the yeast. Leave it alone for 10 minutes, then dissolve the yeast and whip up some froth.
- Put some oil in the pan, some flour, and some salt. Irreconcilable differences must be kept apart.
- Start the bread machine once you've programmed it to make white bread. (The baking time is around three hours.)
- Eat your fill!
- There is a significant decrease in density in white bread made at home.
- Water, 1 cup plus 3 teaspoons Two Tablespoons of Oil, Veggie
- 1/2 a teaspoon of salt Sugar, to taste, 2 tablespoons
- The equivalent of three cups of all-purpose flour
- Use 2 tsp. of dried active yeast
- Put the water and oil in the bread pan. Add sugar to the water and stir. Put some flour in a pot.
- Make a small depression in the top of the flour and keep the ingredients from touching the flour. Spread the yeast in the depression.
- It's important to avoid getting yeast into the water.
- Press the pan down into the bread machine. Lock the lid down.
- Set the bread maker to make a 1.5-pound loaf of basic bread with a medium crust (3 hrs. 15 minutes)
- The bread is done when the pan can be removed easily from the oven without burning your hands. Shaking the bread pan over down causes the loaf to fall out. Place the loaf on a wire rack to cool for 30 minutes.

Peasant Bread Bakery Machine

Cooking Time: 40 Minutes
Servings: 2
Nutritional Analysis:

Calories: 164

Total Fat: 5 g

Carbohydrates: 27g

Fiber: 1.5g

Ingredients:

- yeast, by the tablespoonful
- two and a half cups of all-purpose flour 1/4 cup plus 1 1/2 teaspoons sugar a single table spoon of salt
- 7/8 ounce of liquid
- The use of olive oil as a finishing touch grains like cornmeal, poppy seeds, or sesame seeds
- **Instructions:**
- Follow the bread machine's instructions for adding yeast, flour, sugar, salt, and water.
- Choose the light crust option and a regular loaf size.
- Let the bread rest in the oven for 5 minutes after baking is complete. Make sure the bread is cooling on a rack and brush a little olive oil on top.
- then top with cornmeal, sesame seeds, or poppy seeds. Cool thoroughly before cutting into pieces or storing.
- Store in the freezer or at room temperature in an airtight container.

White Bread From The Country Bread Machine

Cooking Time: 50 Minutes
Servings: 4
Nutritional Analysis:

Calories: 180

Total Fat: 3.8 g

Carbohydrates: 28.9 g

Fiber: 2 g

Ingredients:

- Three-quarters of a cup of room temperature water 2 12 cup of all-purpose flour 1/4 pound of yeast 1 cup of bread flour
- a pinch of baking soda
- 1/3 of a teaspoon of active dry yeast A combination of olive oil and water, equaling 1 tablespoon and 1 teaspoon
- 12 tsp sugar and 1 tsp salt

Instructions:

- Put everything in the bread pan in the order recommended by the manufacturer of your bread maker.

- Select the medium crust option and either the rapid or moderate timer.
- Transfer the bread to a cooling rack.
- Make some cuts and have a good time!

Chapter 7: Sourdough Breads Recipes
Sour Bread, A Modern Craving

Cooking Time: 40 Minutes
Servings: 3
Nutritional Analysis:

Calories: 175

Total Fat: 3.29 g

Carbohydrates: 27.89 g

Fiber: 1.61 g

Ingredients:

- Water, 240 ml (1 cup)
- Exactly one teaspoon of salt
- Produces a loaf weighing around 680 grams (1 pound).
- Culture proof for one cup (240 ml)
- Unbleached all-purpose flour, 34 cup (490 g)

Instructions:

- In a bread pan or other baking container, a willow basket, or, for French loaves, on a baking sheet, place the loaf after it has been formed. Wrap and let rise (at room temperature or in a proofing box's warmer climate, whichever you choose) for two to four hours, or until it's doubled in size or almost the height of the bread pan. Keep in mind that if you proof your bread at a higher temperature (92°C or higher), you may end up with a sourer loaf that has a better taste but less leavening.
- Leavening and sourness may be proofed for intelligence and nuance at room temperature. A little less sweet loaf with only slightly reduced leavening may be achieved by proofing it at room temperature for the first hour and then at ninety (thirty-two) till risen. Repeatedly slash the surface of the dough with a razor blade before placing the bread in the oven. Put the pan containing the formed and proofed bread into a very cold oven, then raise the temperature to 375 degrees Fahrenheit (190 degrees Celsius), and bake for 70 minutes.
- Bake the bread for 40 minutes in a preheated 450°F (230°C) oven on a baking sheet or directly on a baking stone. During the last 15 minutes of baking, spray the inside of the oven with water every 5 minutes or lay a pan of boiling water directly under the loaf. This will produce a crust that is firm and chewy. Please take the bread from the pan and cool on a wire rack for at least 15 to 20 minutes after baking before slicing.

Sourdough Made With Oats, A Unique Bread Recipe

Cooking Time: 30 Minutes
Servings: 1
Nutritional Analysis:

Calories: 158

Total Fat: 3.78 g

Carbohydrates: 28.99 g

Fiber: 1.7 g

Ingredients:

- moderate heat Peel and grate two apples.
- 200 milliliters (1 cup) of rolled oats
- 50% (125 ml) water, one-fourth cup (125 ml) sugar,

Instructions:

- Blend the oats until they are the same consistency as flour. Put everything into a bad glass jar with a tight cover and let it sit for two to four days. An early morning or evening stir inside is recommended. Once the Mixture begins to bubble, it is time to make the starter. All you have to do now is "feed" the dough so it keeps its taste and fermentation potential.
- Feed the sourdough once weekly with half a cup (100 ml) water and one cup (100 g) oat flour if you're keeping it in the fridge. The sourdough starter has to be fed the same way every day if it is to survive being stored at space temperature. There should be enough liquid to make the mixture porridge-like. If you have any extra sourdough, you may try freezing it in 1-cup portions.

Sour Dough Malt

Cooking Time: 50 Minutes
Servings: 4
Nutritional Analysis:

Calories: 188

Total Fat: 3.27g

Carbohydrates: 29.8 g

Fiber: 1.51 g

Ingredients:

- 2 cups of water equal 16 ounces.
- one-fourth cup of canned, evaporated milk
- A couple of tablespoons of honey or malt syrup
- two tablespoons of cooled, melted butter
- the equivalent of 3/4 cup of 100% vigor Rye
- starter for sourdough bread, 6.7 ounce
- Two pounds and four ounces of bread flour, divided into eight cups.

- To season with salt, use 4 teaspoons (or about.8 ounces) (add after dough autolysis)

Instructions:

- Put everything except the salt in the mixer and mix on low for two to three minutes. After that, let the dough autolyze (rest) for twenty minutes.
- After the dough has autolyzed, add the salt and knead it for 5 minutes on a low pace. Gluten development is aided by a longer rise time in bread baked using a one-day mix and bake method. It takes around four hours for the dough to bulk ferment, often called the first rise. During the whole 4-hour bulk fermentation, the dough only has to be mixed down by three rounds of the dough hook, twice.
- For the same reason that folding would, it also helps to align the gluten strands and strengthens them. During bulk ferment, you will also place the dough in a folding dough trough and fold it twice. Rye flours produce a sticky dough.

Soured Potato Bread

Cooking Time: 50 Minutes
Servings: 2
Nutritional Analysis:

Calories: 143

Total Fat: 3.27g

Carbohydrates: 28.89 g

Fiber: 1.1 g

Ingredients:

- The equivalent of two regular potatoes,
- honey, 1 tsp
- 1 tsp of all-purpose flour

Instructions:

- The potatoes should be mixed until they have the consistency of gruel. Mix the honey and the flour within the bowl. Keep the concoction in a large, airtight container. The morning and evening stirring is recommended. Slightly more time is needed to bake sourdough than regular bread. This, however, is a case of appreciating the buffer. Between five and seven days, it will be completed. When bubbles form in the starter, it is done.
- Now all you have to do to keep the dough's taste and fermentation potential intact is "feed" it with Sourdine. To maintain the sourdough starter in the fridge, feed it once a week with a mixture of a half cup (100 ml) of potato gruel and one tbsp of spelled flour. The sourdough starter has to be fed the same amount of flour and water every day at room temperature. The texture should be similar to that of thick porridge. The 0. five-cup capacity of most freezer bags is perfect for storing leftover sourdough.

Sourdough Made With Honey And Whole Grain

Cooking Time: 50 Minutes
Servings: 4
Nutritional Analysis:

Calories: 143

Total Fat: 3.29 g

Carbohydrates: 28g

Fiber: 2 g

Ingredients:

- One kilogram (nine cups) of wheat flour
- 500 milliliters (2 cups) of room temperature water
- Wheat sourdough starter, 12 ounces (350 grams)
- 150 grams (about 2/3 of a cup) of room temperature water
- Just 250 grams (1 cup) of all-purpose flour
- 1/3 to 1/4 teaspoon of active dry yeast (5 g)
- half a tablespoon of honey
- one-tenth of a tablespoon (10 g) of salt

Instructions:

- Combine all of the ingredients, excluding the salt, with the dough made the day before. Salt the dough after it has been kneaded until it has reached an elastic state. Divide the dough in thirds and form the dough into three round loaves.
- After lightly coating the loaves in flour, set them on a baking sheet that has been buttered. Put the bread in the fridge to rise for approximately 10 hours. Bake the loaves for 25 to 30 minutes at 475 degrees Fahrenheit (240 degrees Celsius).

Sourdough Made With Olives And Rosemary

Cooking Time: 30 Minutes
Servings: 1
Nutritional Analysis:

Calories: 193

Total Fat: 6 g

Carbohydrates: 30.89 g

Fiber: 1.1 g

Ingredients:

- 34 teaspoon (10 g) active dry yeast
- A pinch of salt (around 5 grams)
- a tablespoon of olive oil
- eighty grams of wheat flour and one ounce of sourdough starter

- Wheat flour, two cups' worth (250 g)
- 125 milliliters (half a cup) of room temperature water
- Herbs of Rosemary, Just Cut

Instructions:

- Aside from the oil and rosemary, mix all the ingredients together until they form a cohesive dough. Set aside twenty minutes for rising time. Flatten the dough into a rectangle about one-tenth of an inch (three millimeters) thick. Rub some olive oil on your brush. Cut some fresh rosemary sprigs in half and place them on top of the dough. The dough is rolled from the shorter end of the rectangle. Stop the loose ends from spreading. Leave the bread to rise for 30 minutes, then cut a deep slit in the center. As a result, you can see right through to the underlying layers.
- Ten more minutes of rising time should be fine. Turn the oven on to 475 degrees Fahrenheit (250 degrees C). The bread should be baked immediately. The stove bottom needs a cup of water sprinkled on it. Turn the oven down to 400 degrees (210 degrees Celsius), and bake for another 20 minutes. Spread the oil-soaked rosemary leaves out on the oil-brushed dough. The dough is rolled. Grab both ends and pinch them together. When the bread has risen, score it.

Sour Bread In The American Method

Cooking Time: 30 Minutes
Servings: 2
Nutritional Analysis:

Calories: 141

Total Fat: 4 g

Carbohydrates: 28.8 g

Fiber: 1.4 g

Ingredients:

- A pinch of salt, or half a teaspoon
- Water, 240 ml (1 cup)
- Produces a loaf weighing around 680 grams (1 pound).
- A 240-milliliter (one cup) sample from the culture proof.
- Four and a half hundred and ninety grams (3 cups) of all-purpose flour (not bleached)

Instructions:

- Put the lifestyle into a blender and mix it up. Dissolve the salt in the water and include it into your routine. To make a cup (140 g) of flour too thick to consolidate with a spoon, add flour a little at a time. Flip out onto a floured board and knead the dough a few times to incorporate any remaining flour and make a silky-smooth batter. Instead, use a bread machine or similar device to mix and knead all of the ingredients for around 25 minutes.
- After waiting thirty minutes, form the batter into desired shapes. Take a light hand and make it smoother. Then, bring some up from the edges and push it in toward the center. To make a French quantity, roll it about the mixture mass to form a rough ball, then gently tap the batter into an uncomfortable square shape, fold it in half, and squeeze the sides together to form a crease.

- Place the created quantity crease-side down on a prepared sheet and confirm for two to four hours. Proof the quantity at room temperature for the crucial hour, then store it in the refrigerator between 85- and 90-degrees Fahrenheit (29 and 32 degrees Celsius) in a tightly sealed container for the best results on a good Combine of acridity and rising. Place the sheet pan with the measured quantity on a cold burner. At this time, turn the oven up to 375 degrees Fahrenheit (190 degrees Celsius), and cook for 70 minutes. Alternately, transfer the quantity to a preparation stone in a burner prepared to 450 degrees Fahrenheit (230 degrees Celsius) and heat for forty minutes.
- If you want the exterior to be firm and chewy, you may do it by either placing a jar of bubbling water beneath the quantity or spraying the broiler with water every five minutes for 15 minutes. When done, remove the quantity from the container and let it cool on a wire rack for at least 15 to 20 minutes before slicing.

Sourdough With Cheese And Sesame Seeds

Cooking Time: 20 Minutes
Servings: 2
Nutritional Analysis:

Calories: 155

Total Fat: 3 g

Carbohydrates: 28.9 g

Fiber: 1.9 g

Ingredients:

- 350 milliliters (1 cup) of room-temperature water
- A measure of durum wheat flour equal to one cup (or 200 grams)
- Wheat flour, one cup (about 200 grams)
- tablespoon (15 g) salt
- Grated cheese, such Swiss or Emmental, two-fourths cup (250 g)
- Toasted sesame seeds, 1/2 cup (100 ml)
- Wheat sourdough starter, 8 ounces (240 grams)
- 400 grams (about 2/3 cup) of all-purpose flour (amount will vary depending on the cheese used)
- Bowl-side olive oil

Instructions:

- Making ensuring the dough isn't too cold requires taking it out of the fridge early. Include seasoning, dairy, seeds, and flour. If the cheese is on the drier side, you may get away with using less flour. Mix well, then let the dough rise in a highly oiled basin lined with tin foil until it has doubled in size, about an hour. Unfold the dough on a table and carefully divide it into thirds.
- Form into round loaves carefully. Arrange the bread in a single layer on a prepared baking sheet, and let it rise for about 30 minutes. To preheat an oven, set the temperature to 450 degrees Fahrenheit (230 degrees Celsius). Place the bread into the oven and reduce the heat to 400F (210C). Put it in the oven and set the timer for 30 minutes. Sesame seeds are best when toasted in a dry pan. Do not mix the dough until the sesame seeds have cooled.
- Shape the dough into round loaves with great care once it's ready. After 30 minutes, carefully cut the tops of the loaves and dust them with flour; then place them in a preheated oven.

Sourdough Made With Malted Wheat

Cooking Time: 40 Minutes
Servings: 2
Nutritional Analysis:

Calories: 155

Total Fat: 3g

Carbohydrates: 28 g

Fiber: 1 g

Ingredients:

- 4.2 ounces of whole wheat flour is equivalent to one cup.
- Malted rye berries, cracked, half a cup
- Using 100% water, a 9-ounce cup of Deem starting will produce a potent one cup of starter.
- 20 ounces is equal to two and a half cups.
- 7.2 ounces of rye flour, or two cups
- Two and a half tablespoons (about 0.7 ounces) of normal cracked wheat equals half a cup.

Instructions:

- Stir in all ingredients except salt until well combined, then let the mixture sit for 20 minutes (batter autolysis). When the autolysis is complete, add the salt and then mix the ingredients for about three minutes on low speed. After letting the batter rest (first rise) for four to fifty percent drunk hours, dump it onto a lightly dusted (Rye flour) surface and knead it until it forms a ball.
- Allow the batter to rest for five to ten minutes after you've divided and shaped the mixture into the rough shape you require (seat rest). Afterward, form the quantities into their final forms and place them in the bins, container, or Couche that have been lined with wax paper or flour. Inject the Blend with hard evidence for a few hours (till almost multiplied anyway delicate when you press in a finger).
- Prepare using the Roasting Pan Method of steaming by cutting, splashing, and cooking for 20 minutes on top of a heating stone in an oven warmed to 450F/232.2C. After the first 20 minutes, reduce the heat to 400F/204.4C and continue baking for another 15–20 minutes, or until the bread is done.

Freshly Baked White Sourdough Bread

Cooking Time: 30 Minutes
Servings: 2
Nutritional Analysis:

Calories: 156

Total Fat: 5 g

Carbohydrates: 40 g

Fiber: 2 g

Ingredients:

- Unbleached rye flour, about half a cup (50 g) (i.e., flour without wheat)

- glasses (750 ml) of room temperature water
- Six cups of wheat flour (about 750 grams)
- 100 grams of wheat sourdough starter, or 3.50 ounces
- 200 milliliters (1 cup) of room-temperature water
- 1/4 cup of flour (around 150 grams)
- 2 teaspoons (20 grams) of salt

Instructions:

- To make dough, combine the flour with the water. Ensure that the dough is well-kneaded. Use a little salt. A further two minutes of dough kneading is recommended. The dough needs an hour to rise before it can be divided into two loaves.
- A 45-minute cloth rest period is needed for the bread to rise. We started with a temperature of 525 degrees Fahrenheit in the oven (280 degrees Celsius). Turn the oven temperature up to 350 degrees F. Start by setting your oven temperature to 350 degrees Fahrenheit. The bread should be baked. Put a cup of water at the base of the burner.

Sourdough Bread From Asia

Cooking Time: 45 Minutes
Servings: 3
Nutritional Analysis:

Calories: 122

Total Fat: 3.66g

Carbohydrates: 28.9 g

Fiber: 1.6 g

Ingredients:

- Wheat sourdough starter, 8 fluid ounces (150 grams)
- tablespoon (15 g) salt
- raw sugar, 1 tbsp
- twenty grams (3/4 ounce) of active yeast
- 300 milliliters (one-fourth cup) of room-temperature water
- Whole wheat flour equivalent to 54 cup (650 g)
- a quarter of a cup (50 ml) of olive oil
- brushed with melted butter

Instructions:

- Dissolve the yeast in a little bit of water. Knead the ingredients together in a big Combining basin. If you find you need more water than is specified, try adding it a bit at a time.
- This is just an estimate, however, due to the fact that the reactivity of flour varies. After the dough has been kneaded, shape it into a loaf and cover it with a clean kitchen towel; let it rest in a warm place for 45 minutes to an hour.

Sour Yeast Bread

Cooking Time: 40 Minutes
Servings: 3
Nutritional Analysis:

Calories: 173

Total Fat: 3.28 g

Carbohydrates: 28.89 g

Fiber: 1.1 g

Ingredients:

- 100 milliliters (50 ml) of ambient temperature water
- Fine rye flour equivalent to six cups (625 g)
- 1/3 to 1/4 cup wheat flour (225 g)
- Sourdough starter, spelt out, 35 ounces (1 kilogram)
- tablespoon (15 g) salt
- tablespoons (25 grams) active yeast
- a half tablespoon (35 ml) of treacle syrup (can be substituted with dark syrup)

Instructions:

- A 30-minute rise time is recommended after properly combining the ingredients. Lightly flour a work surface and form the dough into two oblong loaves.
- Tend the bread until it doubles in size (let them grow in a basket, if possible). Turn the oven temperature up to 475 degrees F. (250 degrees Celsius). After brushing the oven with water, put the loaves inside.

A Sourdough Makes With Eastern Wheat

Cooking Time: 35 Minutes
Servings: 2
Nutritional Analysis:

Calories: 143

Total Fat: 3.29g

Carbohydrates: 28 g

Fiber: 5 g

Ingredients:

- the equivalent of one teaspoon of black molasses
- half a cup of rye flour
- Two and a third cups (about 9.7 ounces) of whole wheat flour
- A total of four-and-a-half teaspoons One pound of bread flour 4.30 Grams
- Strong sourdough starter, 2 cups (about 18 ounces)
- 14 cup of lukewarm water (about 14 ounces)
- A Measure of Dry Milk

- equals one ounce of oil to two tablespoons
- Malt syrup, one tablespoon
- Three-quarters of a teaspoon (.7 ounce) of salt (add after dough autolysis)

Instructions:

- Follow autolysis with the addition of salt and a few minutes of low-speed consolidation. Next, wait 6-8 hours before attempting to use the batter. Through the vi - eight-hour mass maturation or crease batter in a battery box, mix the batter down with just three revolutions of the mixture snare.
- It helps to prevent the Mixture from deteriorating too quickly by reinforcing and aligning the gluten strands. The finished mass is poured onto a lightly floured (Whole Wheat flour) surface, where it is worked a few times before gathering into a ball. Split the batter in half.
- Set up the final system with the right proportions and the batter may take a five-to-ten-minute break (seat rest). Form the parts into their final configurations and place them in the hermetic containers (banners are not need to be lined). The batter should be allowed to line out for half an hour before being refrigerated.
- If the batter is too enthused today, you may avoid waiting the required thirty minutes. Dispose of the quantities at staggered thirty-minute intervals the next morning (so that you don't have to do it all at once). At this stage, you may stop sealing and let the batter rise to the top. After resting for an hour to three hours, the batter will have grown around 1.5 times its initial size.

Sour Dough With Carrots And Milk

Cooking Time: 30 Minutes
Servings: 2
Nutritional Analysis:

Calories: 192

Total Fat: 6 g

Carbohydrates: 30 g

Fiber: 3g

Ingredients:

- 100 grams (1 cup) of rolled oats (dry roast them in a non-stick frying pan)
- Wheat sourdough starter, 8 fluid ounces (150 grams)
- 200 milliliters (1 cup) of room-temperature water
- One hundred milliliters (50 ml) of cold milk
- 1/3 to 1/4 teaspoon (5 g) active dry yeast
- tablespoon (15 g) salt
- 3 1/4 cups (450 g) whole wheat flour
- shredded carrots — 2 cups (250 grams)

Instructions:

- Whisk the yeast and milk together. Mix everything together, except the carrots. Take around 10 minutes to knead the dough. Mix in the grated carrots and continue working the dough. You should let the dough 60-90 minutes to rise in a warm area.

- Keep in mind that the dough can cling a little bit. It's important to knead the dough one more once it's finished rising. Put half the dough into two or three oiled pans. Make sure to let the dough 45 minutes to rise. This time is approximate; the dough is ready when it has doubled in bulk. To preheat the oven, set the thermostat to 475 degrees Fahrenheit (250 degrees Celsius). Put the bread in the oven and bake it for ten minutes.
- Bake for a further 30 minutes at 350 degrees Fahrenheit (180 degrees C). Prepare the oats for roasting in a pan that won't stick at all. Ten minutes of vigorous dough-kneading is recommended. Incorporate the grated carrot. The fermented and sloppy dough should fill the pans about halfway.

Sourdough Made With Dark Beer

Cooking Time: 20 Minutes
Servings:
Nutritional Analysis:

Calories: 150

Total Fat: 3.6 g

Carbohydrates: 28 g

Fiber: 1 g

Ingredients:

- Dark Molasses, one Tablespoonful (.7 oz. / 19.8 g)
- Toasted onion flakes, dry, three tablespoons (.6 ounces/17 grams)
- Approximately one ounce (28 grams) of caraway seeds, which is three tablespoons' worth.
- Bread flour (13.5 ounces/382.3 grams) for 3 cups
- Rye starter, two cups full (equaling 18 ounces or 510 grams)
- Six ounces (or 170 grams) is the equivalent of one cup of water.
- Approximately 340 grams (12 ounces) of a delicious black beer.
- Three Tablespoons of Oil (1.50 oz./42 g)
- .8 ounces (22 grams) of non-diastatic malt syrup (1 tablespoon).
- Whole Wheat Flour (12.6 oz / 357 g) for 3 Cups
- Rye flour (for two cups), 7.2 ounces (or 204 grams)
- Four Tablespoons (.8 Ounces/22.7g) of Sea Salt

Instructions:

- The process of combining the ingredients on a medium speed takes around three minutes. Allow the batter to autolyze (relax) for 20 minutes. Until the mass ages (which is the main climb), it will take four to six hours. When you're done, dump the mixture onto a surface lightly dusted with flour (Rye flour), and knead it into a ball a few times.
- The batter should be split in half by a huge chasm. Form the ingredients into the desired shape, then let the Mixture five minutes to rest (seat rest). After the structural quantities have been sidelined (relaxed) into their final bodies, place them in the sealing bushels or containers, lining them with sealing fabrics if necessary (bannetons are not required to be lined). Keep refrigerated for the time being. Allow the batter to warm up and check the next morning after you've discarded the Mixture, staggered it for 40 minutes, and then separated it. When the batter increases in volume by a significant amount, that's when the readings should stabilize.

- When baking with Rye bread, additional caution must be used to prevent the loaves from being over proofed. When the batter is ready and feels bubbly and springy but not droopy, you take the middle portion, sprinkle the top (really the underside) with semolina or whole grain flour, and turn the batter out onto a strip of flat heating sheet. The next step is to cut the batter while it's still on the strip, place it on a hot, warmed baking stone in an oven set to 450F/232.2C, quickly sprinkle the Mixture with water once, and then cover it with a boiling top that has been preheated in the broiler. Put it on high heat for twenty minutes. After 20 minutes, fire up the stove and reduce the temperature of the broiler to 400F/204.4C. Keep baking until a bread thermometer registers 200°F (205°C) (around 18–25 minutes, depending on your oven).
- Halfway during the last searing preparation time, switch the quantity. Cool. Turn on the broiler, save a second copy, and return the simmering cover to the oven to warm for 5 to 10 minutes, or until the final product is ready to go in. Melt the same amount as the real thing. Chill the bread and enjoy it with some late spread or cream cheese. Sandwiches made with It Bread are delicious and have a drab, harsh taste.

Traditional Mexican Sour Dough

Cooking Time: 30 Minutes
Servings: 2
Nutritional Analysis:

Calories: 153

Total Fat: 3.29 g

Carbohydrates: 28.8 g

Fiber: 1.15 g

Ingredients:

- potatoes, mashed, 4 ounces
- One pound and fourteen ounces, or six and a half cups, of bread flour.
- 18 ounces of sourdough starter, or 2 cups, at 166% hydration.
- One-quarter cup of water, or 14 ounces
- Oil: two tablespoons = one ounces
- Honey or malt syrup, one tablespoon (.8 ounces)
- The equivalent of two and a half cups of whole wheat flour is two and a half ounces.
- 1 Tablespoon (4 tsp) =.8 Ounces

Instructions:

- Mix the ingredients together on a low to medium speed until they are well combined. Two minutes is about right for this. At this time, you may let the batter to autolyze (rest) for twenty minutes. When the autolysis is complete, the batter should be slowed down to a low pace for around a minute. The bulk of the combination has to age (which means the primary ascent) for four to five hours before it may be multiplied. During the majority of the fermentation time, when the gluten strands are being formed and aligned, flip the mixture over at least twice.
- To try it, hit the beginning catcher and let the snare spin the batter all the way around the bowl. After the dough has had enough time to rise, dump it out onto a lightly floured surface and knead it into a ball in many separate sessions. Put together the ingredients in about the form you desire, then let the Mixture sit for 10 minutes (seat rest). After putting items on hold, you should mold them into their final forms and place them in lined sealing boxes (Bannetons aren't need to be lined).

- Give the Mixture thirty minutes to come to room temperature before covering it with plastic wrap and placing it in the fridge. Allow the batter to definite evidence for about two hours in the morning (the Mixture may seem multiplied and supple/springy), then turn the Mixture out into a strip and slice, splash, cowl with broiling cover, and cook in a very hot, prepared 450F/232C degree oven for twenty minutes. After 20 minutes, take it off the stovetop and put it under a 400F/204.4C broiler for another 10-15 minutes, flipping often to sear.
- Withdraw a sum and let it all hang out on the rack. If the first quantity is too brown, reduce the broiler temperature to 425F/218.3C for the remaining half of the cooking time. Just before adding the next measure, place the broiling top back in the oven and heat until it reaches 450 degrees. It might be an excellent, tasty quantity, especially when combined with spread or used to make sandwiches.

A Loaf Of Cheddar Sourdough

Cooking Time: 35 Minutes
Servings: 3
Nutritional Analysis:

Calories: 153

Total Fat: 3.98 g

Carbohydrates: 28 g

Fiber: 1.5 g

Ingredients:

- a pinch of kosher salt and two tablespoons of unsalted butter
- Shredded, mild Cheddar cheese (4 ounces).
- You'll need a cup of raw corn kernels,
- Approximately one cup of water at room temperature
- There should be four teaspoons of active dry yeast
- Two teaspoons of salt
- The equivalent of three cups (1312 ounces) of sourdough flour, plus more if necessary

Instructions:

- A cooking spray that is not currently in stock
- Water, yeast, sugar, flour, salt, and margarine should be combined and plied until smooth, either by hand (join in a too large bowl, then flip out and massage) or in a Stand Mixer outfitted with the mixture snare. After this, the batter will be properly strengthened. Toss in the cheddar and corn and mix gently until combined. The moisture within the corn will cause the batter to seem wet and untidy at first, but as the corn cooks and fuses, the batter will become softer and firmer.
- Set the bowl in a warm place for an hour with the lid on, and then check on it to see whether the Mixture has risen to the top. Prepare a nine-by-five-inch amount skillet by showering it with water. Pat the Mixture into a tough 8-inch square after turning it out onto a floured surface. One technique is to push down directly on the edge while overlapping the top so that it is about in the center of the batter's attention. Repeat the prime again and over. It draws attention to the lower one or two inches or so.
- Seal the edge by pressing down. Now, close the crease by pulling the bottom of the batter up to meet the mixture roll you've produced. Squeeze the top and bottom together, then drop the batter into the prepared baking dish, crease side down. Wrap the skillet with saran wrap, or place the whole container inside a large

plastic bag, and knot the bag's open end to seal it. Keep chilled for at least an hour and up to 24 hours before cooking. After around 6 hours, the mixture should begin to rise.

Danish Sensory Bread

Cooking Time: 45 Minutes
Servings: 2
Nutritional Analysis:

Calories: 183

Total Fat: 3.29 g

Carbohydrates: 28 g

Fiber: 1.15 g

Ingredients:

- 7.2 ounces (204 grams) of dark rye flour is equivalent to two cups.
- False Front 8.4 ounces/238 grams of Whole Wheat Flour
- 13.5 oz. (382 g) Bread Flour, Three Profiles
- In order to make a strong starting for Danish Rye, you will need two cups of 100% hydrated starter.
- Approximately 16 ounces (453 grams) of coffee is plenty for two cups.
- The equivalent of 1.5 ounces (42 grams) of oil is 3 tablespoons.
- The equivalent of one.4 ounces (39.7 grams) of molasses is two tablespoons.
- Three.5-ounce (14.0g) teaspoons of salt

Instructions:

- Just until combined, combine all ingredients with salt and let the batter rest for 20 minutes (autolyze). Turn the speed down to low and continue mixing for a few minutes after autolysis. After then, give the mass of the combination time to develop (the first ascent) for six hours. When the dough is ready, turn it out onto a surface dusted with fine flour (Rye flour) and knead it until it forms a ball.
- The Mixture was divided into two enormous piles, each weighing in at little over three pounds. Each. Mold dough into a rough form, then let it rest for five to ten minutes (seat rest). While waiting, form the remaining quantities into their final forms and transfer them to the storage containers, the frying pan, or the Couche. Place banneton in plastic bag and store in the fridge. In the morning, let the Mixture sit out for two to two and a half hours (until essentially multiplied anyway delicate when you press during a finger), at that point slice, shower, and cook, on top of a heating stone, in a preheated 450F/232.2C degree stove for twenty minutes utilizing the Roasting Pan Method for steaming.
- After the first twenty minutes, reduce the broiler temperature to 400F/204.4C and continue cooking for an additional 18 to 25 minutes, or until a bread thermometer inserted into the center registers 200 205F/93 96C. Cool. It has the potential to be a healthy, palatable, and well-freezable improved rye.

Sour Bread With Milk Grains

Cooking Time: 45 Minutes
Servings: 2
Nutritional Analysis:

Calories: 160

Total Fat: 4 g

Carbohydrates: 28 g

Fiber: 1.5 g

Ingredients:

- Millet seed, 1 tbsp (.4 oz)
- a quarter cup of flax seeds, or 0.5 ounces
- It takes 8 ounces of boiling water to fill a standard measuring cup.
- Mixture of cracked wheat and rye, 6 ounces (1 cup)
- Malt syrup, one table spoon (.8 ounces)
- .4 ounces (1 tablespoon) sesame or dill seeds
- a quarter cup of sunflower seeds or 1.5 ounces of a seed/trail mix

Instructions:

- If you use more than the recommended number of seeds, you'll need to adjust the other liquid ingredients, such as water or flour, to make up the difference. Let the mixture autolyze for 20 minutes after being stirred for two to three minutes inside the mixer. Next, whisk in the cooled seed/grain mixture and the salt to the batter. Let the Blend sit for about 6 hours to allow for maximum mass maturation. Fold the variety at regular intervals throughout the massage.
- When the bulk ferment is complete, gently press down the batter and transfer it to a rye dusted work surface. Use just enough force to form a ball by working the batter. To make two loaves of bread, divide the mixture in half and mold the dough into loaves. Put the dough in bushels that have been dusted with flour or lined with plastic wrap and put them in the fridge. Take the ingredients out of the fridge the day before (you won't believe the difference 30 minutes can make) and allow the Mixture get to room temperature before you try it.
- Due of the high seed content of It Bread, the Mixture may take longer to provide evidence (anticipate that it should take a couple of-three hours or extra). When the mixture is well-combined and feels bubbly and springy but not droopy, scoop out a small portion, dust the top (actually the base) with semolina or rye flour, and flip the batter out onto a strip of flat heating sheet.
- After the Mixture has been sliced while still on the strip, it is placed into a hot heating stone in a fresh oven warmed to 450 degrees Fahrenheit (232 degrees Celsius), the batter is quickly sprayed with water, and the dish is covered with a broiling cover.

Traditional Spicy Jalapeno Bread

Cooking Time: 35 Minutes
Servings: 2
Nutritional Analysis:

Calories: 155

Total Fat: 3.9 g

Carbohydrates: 28.8 g

Fiber: 1.5 g

Ingredients:

- Rye flour, one ounce (about half a cup)
- One package (two cups) of bread flour, 9 ounces
- The moisture level of a healthy sourdough starter is 16 percent, which equates to 9 ounces of dough in one cup.
- There are 12 ounces in a half cup.
- Two-thirds of a cup of whole wheat flour.
- an Ounce

Instructions:

- Combine all of the ingredients, including the salt, and set aside for 20 minutes. Wait four to six hours, or multiply by ten, for confirmation. Get Jalapeno cheddar that is around 8 ounces in a block. Put the batter into two separate bowls.
- Unfold a single square of the Mixture and push four ounces of the jumbled cheddar into the batter to make a rectangle. Now divide the batter into thirds horizontally. Flatten the batter once more, sprinkle the other 4 ounces of cheddar on top, and fold in thirds. After five minutes, finish shaping the Mixture by bending down and compressing the batter at the base to get the desired quantity. Place dollops of batter in a greased bread pan or a banneton/crate.
- Assemble various quantities, and then let them rest for two to three hours, or until the batter has increased in bulk by about a factor of 1.5. 69 Next, cut the batter while it's still on the strip, place it on a hot heating stone in a fresh oven warmed to 400F/204.2C, quickly sprinkle the Mixture with water, and cover it with a simmering lid.
- Plan on spending the next twenty minutes getting ready. The bread is done when a thermometer inserted into the center reads between 200- and 205-degrees Fahrenheit (93 and 96 degrees Celsius) and the broiler cover has been removed after 20 minutes. During the last ten minutes of prepping and cooking, turn the quantity half way. Cool. After that, you need to turn on the broiler, make a second copy, and put the simmering top back in the oven to warm for 5-10 minutes, depending on how much food you have to put in.

Chapter 8: Fruits Bread Recipes

Highest Quality Whole Wheat Sliceable Bread For Snacks

Cooking Time: 50 Minutes
Servings: 4
Nutritional Analysis:

Calories: 180

Total Fat: 3.8 g

Carbohydrates: 28.9 g

Fiber: 2 g

Ingredients:

- Light buttermilk, 3 cups plus 2 teaspoons Amount: 2 tbsp dry milk
- Three Tablespoons of Local Honey
- A couple of teaspoons of pure olive oil
- 1 and 3/4 teaspoons of all-purpose white flour 1 and 14 kilos of bread yeast
- baking powder, salt, and yeast in tablespoons

Instructions:

- Prepare the bread machine by placing the ingredients in the order specified.
- Since the yeast doesn't interact with the liquid below, it's crucial that you place it in a tiny well in the flour if you're not going to be making the bread straight away thanks to the delay timer.
- Prepare in accordance with the manufacturer's instructions.

Typical White Bread

Cooking Time: 50 Minutes
Servings: 2
Nutritional Analysis:

Calories: 195

Total Fat: 5.8 g

Carbohydrates: 30g

Fiber: 2.1g

Ingredients:

- You get 8 pieces for every pound.
- 3/4 cup water, between 80 and 90 degrees
- spoonful of cooled melted butter One tablespoon of sugar and three-quarters of a teaspoon of salt the equivalent of 2 teaspoons of nonfat dry milk
- cups all-purpose flour
- 1/3 of a teaspoon of active dry yeast (or instant yeast) A dozen slices/one and a half pounds
- A cup and an eighth, between 80- and 90-degrees Fahrenheit

- Melted butter (1 1/2 tablespoons), cooled One and a half teaspoons of sugar and one teaspoon of salt Requirements: 3 tbsp. of fat-free milk powder
- Three cups of all-purpose flour
- 16 pieces of bread, approximately 2 pounds, and 114 teaspoons of instant or bread machine yeast.
- One and a half cups of water, between eighty and ninety degrees
- 2 teaspoons of cooled melted butter
- Mix together 2 tablespoons of sugar and 2 teaspoons of salt.
- 14 cup of nonfat dry milk powder + 4 cups of all-purpose flour 1 1/2 teaspoons of yeast (either active dry yeast or instant)

Instructions:

- Prepare your bread machine as directed by the manufacturer and add the ingredients.
- Select between a light or medium crust and click Start after setting the bread maker to the Basic/White bread setting.
- As soon as the bread is done baking, take the bucket out of the appliance.
- The bread should rest for 5 minutes after baking.
- Shake the bucket to loosen the loaf, then turn it out onto a cooling rack.

Whole-Wheat Bread With Honey

Cooking Time: 40 Minutes
Servings: 3
Nutritional Analysis:

Calories: 150

Total Fat: 3 g

Carbohydrates: 28 g

Fiber: 1.11 g

Ingredients:

- You get 8 pieces for every pound.
- 3/4 cup water, between 80- and 90-degrees Honey, 1 Tablespoon
- spoonful of cooled melted butter
- 1/2 tsp. salt
- cups of all-purpose flour
- a half cup of all-purpose flour
- 12 slices/1.25 pounds of bread = 1 teaspoon of bread machine yeast or quick yeast.
- 80°F to 90°F water, 1/8 cup 1 cup water 2 teaspoons honey
- Melted butter (1 1/2 tablespoons), cooled
- 1/4 tsp. salt
- Two and a half cups of whole wheat flour
- 14 cup all-purpose flour
- 112 teaspoons of yeast (either dry active yeast from a bread machine or quick yeast) 2 pounds of flour 16 slices of bread

- One and a half cups of water, between eighty and ninety degrees You'll need 3 teaspoons of honey.
- three tablespoons of melted butter one teaspoon of salt
- 3.14 cups of whole wheat flour White flour for bread, one cup
- 2-tablespoons of yeast, either active dry yeast or instant

Instructions:

- Prepare your bread machine as directed by the manufacturer and add the ingredients.
- Select between a light or medium crust and click Start after setting the bread maker to the Basic/White bread setting.
- As soon as the bread is done baking, take the bucket out of the appliance.
- The bread should rest for 5 minutes after baking.
- Shake the bucket to loosen the loaf, then turn it out onto a cooling rack.

Breads Made From Molasses Wheat

Cooking Time: 30 Minutes
Servings: 2
Nutritional Analysis:

Calories: 163

Total Fat: 3 g

Carbohydrates: 35g

Fiber: 2.5 g

Ingredients:

- You get 8 pieces for every pound.
- 12 cup water, between 80 and 90 degrees
- A quarter cup of milk, heated to 80 degrees
- 2 tablespoons honey 2 teaspoons melted butter, cooled
- 1/4 teaspoon of molasses
- Exactly One Tablespoon of Sugar
- 1/4 teaspoon of nonfat dry milk
- 1/2 tsp. salt
- 1/4 of a cup of unsweetened cocoa powder 1 1/4 cups of all-purpose flour
- White flour for bread, one cup
- 12 slices/1.25 pounds of bread = 1 teaspoon of bread machine yeast or quick yeast.
- 80°F to 90°F water, 3/4 cup Approximately a third of a cup of milk heated to 80 degrees
- 4 tablespoons of honey 1 tablespoon of cooled melted butter
- spoonsful of molasses
- Two tablespoons of sugar
- The equivalent of 2 teaspoons of nonfat dry milk
- 1/4 tsp. salt
- 1 cup of skim milk 2 tablespoons of unsweetened cocoa powder Thirteen and a half cups of whole wheat flour

- 1.5 cups all-purpose flour
- 16 slices/ 2 pounds of bread; 1 1/8 teaspoons of yeast (either active dry yeast or instant yeast).

Instructions:

- cup of water, between 80- and 90-degrees Fahrenheit
- A half cup of milk at room temperature (around 80 degrees Fahrenheit)
- five teaspoons honey five tablespoons cooled melted butter
- spoonsful of molasses
- 1.5 grams of sugar
- Requirements: 3 tbsp. of fat-free milk powder 1/2-gram sugar 1 gram fat 1 gram protein 1 teaspoon salt
- cup of sugar or honey Two and a half cups of whole wheat flour
- cups all-purpose flour
- 1 1/2 tablespoons bread machine or instant yeast
- Prepare your bread machine as directed by the manufacturer and add the ingredients.

Instructions:

- Select between a light or medium crust and click Start after setting the bread maker to the Basic/White bread setting.
- As soon as the bread is done baking, take the bucket out of the appliance.
- The bread should rest for 5 minutes after baking.
- Shake the bucket to loosen the loaf, then turn it out onto a cooling rack.
- Ingredient Pro Tip: Unsulfured molasses is sweeter and doesn't have that subtle chemical flavor as sulfured molasses does. In addition, light molasses is not as good as the dark or blackstrap kind while making this bread.

Whole-Wheat Bread Only

Cooking Time: 45 Minutes
Servings:
Nutritional Analysis:

Calories: 200

Total Fat: 3.5 g

Carbohydrates: 3g

Fiber: 2.5g

Ingredients:

- Eight quarters per pound, three-quarters of a cup of water between eighty and ninety degrees
- 1 1/2 teaspoons of honey, 1 1/2 tablespoons of melted butter, cooled
- 1/4 teaspoon of salt
- Bread flour, whole wheat, 2 cups
- You can make 12 slices of bread out of 1 1/2 pounds of dough with only 1 teaspoon of instant yeast or yeast from a bread machine.
- 80°F to 90°F water, 1 1/8 cups
- Two and a half teaspoons of melted butter, two and a half tablespoons of honey, cooled
- 1.182 grams of salt

- Bread flour (3 cups whole wheat)
- 2 pounds of flour 16 slices of bread 1.2 teaspoons of active dry yeast
- 120 ml of water, between 80 and 90 degrees
- Three teaspoons of honey, three tablespoons of melted butter, and three tablespoons of each to cool
- 2 tablespoons of salt
- 334 cups of 100% whole wheat flour for bread

Instructions:

- Bread machine yeast or instant yeast, 2 tablespoons
- Put everything into the bread maker as directed.
- Select a light or medium crust and click Start to bake whole-wheat/whole-grain bread in a bread machine.
- At the end of the baking process, take the bucket out of the appliance.
- It's best to wait 5 minutes before cutting into the bread.
- In order to get the loaf out of the bucket, give it a little shake, and then flip it over onto a cooling rack.

Crunchy French Bread

Cooking Time: 30 Minutes
Servings: 2
Nutritional Analysis:

Calories: 163

Total Fat: 6g

Carbohydrates: 20g

Fiber: 1 g

Ingredients:

- One pound is eight slices.
- 80°F to 90°F water, about 2/3 cup Two Tablespoons of Olive Oil
- teaspoons of salt and sugar
- bread flour
- 1 tsp. instant yeast or bread machine yeast
- A dozen slices/one and a half pounds
- cup of water, between 80- and 90-degrees Fahrenheit Almost a Tablespoon of Olive Oil
- 2 tablespoons sugar 1 1/4 teaspoons salt
- bread flour
- 114 teaspoons of dry yeast or 12 teaspoon of instant yeast 16 slices/ 2 pounds
- 114 cups water, between 80 and 90 degrees 2 Tablespoons of Olive Oil
- 2 tbsp sugar 112 tsp salt
- Four Cups of All-Purpose Flour
- 1 1/2 teaspoons of yeast (either dry or instant)

Instructions:

- Put everything into the bread maker as directed.
- Set the machine to bake French bread, choose a crust setting (light or medium), and hit Start.

- At the end of the baking process, take the bucket out of the appliance.
- It's best to wait 5 minutes before cutting into the bread.
- In order to get the loaf out of the bucket, give it a little shake, and then flip it over onto a cooling rack.

A White Bread For Any And Every Occasion

Cooking Time: 25 Minutes
Servings: 2
Nutritional Analysis:

Calories: 163

Total Fat: 3g

Carbohydrates: 28 g

Fiber: 1g

Ingredients:

- Water temperature of 80 degrees Fahrenheit, or 3/4 cup
- butter, melted, 1 tablespoon sugar
- 1/4 teaspoon of salt
- skim milk powder (about 4 teaspoons' worth) Two Cups All-Purpose Flour
- 1/4 teaspoon of dry yeast

Instructions:

- To use a bread machine, put all the ingredients in the pan and then turn it on, following the manufacturer's instructions.
- Program your bread maker for Basic/White Bread and choose the medium crust setting.
- To begin, please press the "start" button.
- Don't do anything till the cycle is finished.
- When the loaf is done baking, remove the bucket and set the bread aside to cool for 5 minutes.
- To get the loaf out of the bucket, give it a little shake.
- Move to a wire rack to cool, then cut and serve.

Bread With A Generally Appreciated Mustard Flavor

Cooking Time: 35Minutes
Servings: 4
Nutritional Analysis:

Calories: 163

Total Fat: 3.8 g

Carbohydrates: 28.9 g

Fiber: 1.15 g

Ingredients:

- 1 1/4 cups milk
- Sunflower milk, 3 Tablespoons Three teaspoons of sour cream
- Approximately 2 teaspoons of dry mustard 1, beaten, entire egg
- 1/2 vanilla sugar sachet Quantity of Flour Needed: 4 Cups
- Yeast and sugar, 1 teaspoon and 2 teaspoons
- 1 ounce of salt

Instructions:

- To prepare bread, remove the bread maker's bucket and add milk, sunflower oil, sour cream, and an egg that has been beaten.
- Combine the sugar, salt, flour, mustard powder, and vanilla sugar.
- Create an indentation in the flour and drop the yeast into it.
- Then, cover the bread maker's bucket and transfer the contents.
- Program your bread maker for Basic/White Bread and choose the medium crust setting.
- To begin, please press the "start" button.
- Don't do anything till the cycle is finished.
- When the loaf is done baking, remove the bucket and set the bread aside to cool for 5 minutes.
- To get the loaf out of the bucket, give it a little shake.
- Place on a cooling rack, then cut into slices and serve.

Traditional White Bread From The Country

Cooking Time: 40 Minutes
Servings: 2
Nutritional Analysis:

Calories: 173

Total Fat: 3.0 g

Carbohydrates: 28g

Fiber: 1g

Ingredients:

- Amounts: 12 tablespoon sugar 2 teaspoons active dry yeast
- 4 cups all-purpose flour the ingredients are: 12 teaspoon of salt 1 big egg
- 1 1/2 teaspoons of margarine
- one cup of milk at a temperature between 43 and 46 degrees Celsius (110- and 115-degrees Fahrenheit).

Instructions:

- The liquids should be combined and added to the pan. Put in all the dry ingredients except the yeast. Make a well in the center of the dry ingredients by pressing down with your hand. Simply drop the yeast into the opening.
- Closing the cover on the chamber after inserting the pan will keep the heat in. Pick the default configuration and the crust color you like most. To begin, please press the "start" button.
- After the bread has finished baking, place it on a wire cooling rack. Prepare slices after cooling.

Bread With Anadama

Cooking Time: 40 Minutes
Servings: 4
Nutritional Analysis:

Calories: 148

Total Fat: 4 g

Carbohydrates:30 g

Fiber: 2g

Ingredients:

- 1/4 cup pumpkin seeds
- 1.5 grams instant yeast 4 and a half cups of all-purpose flour
- 1/4 cup of cornmeal, yellow
- 1 1/2 teaspoons of salt 2 tablespoons of diced unsalted butter
- 1/4 cup of powdered skim milk
- a quarter cup of molasses
- 1.25 cups water, between 80- and 90-degrees Fahrenheit (26 and 32 degrees Celsius)

Instructions:

- Besides the sunflower seeds, add the following to the pan: water, molasses, milk, salt, butter, cornmeal, flour, and yeast.
- Put the dish in the microwave and shut the door.
- Sunflower seeds, please place in the fruit and nut dispensing machine.
- Activate the device and adjust the primary knob to your preferred crust color. To begin, please press the "start" button.

Chapter 9: Spice & Nut Bread Recipes
Bread Made With Oats And Apricots

Cooking Time: 45 Minutes
Servings: 3
Nutritional Analysis:

Calories: 180

Total Fat: 3g

Carbohydrates: 40g

Fiber: 4g

Ingredients:

- 4 1/4 cups all-purpose flour About two-thirds of a cup of rolled oats
- Approximately 1 tbsp of white sugar
- You'll need: 1 tsp. of dry active yeast, 1.5 tsp. of salt
- 1 tsp of cinnamon powder 1-2/3 cups orange juice 2 Tbsp. of diced butter
- 1/2 cup of dried apricots, chopped
- 2 teaspoons of heated honey

Instructions:

- Place all of the bread ingredients in the pan of the bread machine, following the manufacturer's instructions. Then, before the last phase of the kneading cycle, include the dried apricots.
- Take the bread out of the bread machine as soon as it's done baking, then brush it with honey that has been warmed in the microwave. Let cool fully before serving.

Fantastic Bread, Made With Love At Home

Cooking Time: 40 Minutes
Servings: 3
Nutritional Analysis:

Calories: 143

Total Fat: 4.8 g

Carbohydrates: 38.89 g

Fiber: 3.9 g

Ingredients:

- 2 and 1/2 tablespoons of dried active yeast
- 1-fourth cup of hot (above 45 degrees Celsius) water Approximately 1 tbsp of white sugar
- a total of 4 cups of all-purpose flour
- Dry Potato Flakes, 14 Cup
- The equivalent of a quarter cup of dry milk powder Salt, to taste, 2 tablespoons
- 1/4 cup white sugar
- 1 stick of butter 2 teaspoons of margarine
- 1 cup of room temperature water (around 100 degrees Fahrenheit or 45 degrees Celsius)

Instructions:

- After you've mixed the yeast, sugar, and 1/4 cup of warm water, let the mixture rest for 15 minutes.
- Gather all of the ingredients, including the yeast, and place them in the bread machine's pan in the order specified by the manufacturer. Select the most fundamental, minimally crusty options.

Freshly Bake White Bread With Honey

Cooking Time: 30 Minutes
Servings: 2
Nutritional Analysis:

Calories: 193

Total Fat: 3.2 g

Carbohydrates: 28.9 g

Fiber: 3g

Ingredients:

- 1 glass milk
- 2 tablespoons honey and 3 teaspoons of melted unsalted butter
- Bread flour equivalent to three cups
- 1/4 teaspoon of salt
- 34 teaspoon of vitamin C powder
- 1/2 gram of dried ginger

Instructions:

- Active dry yeast equal to 1 1/2 teaspoons
- Put the ingredients in the bread maker in the sequence specified by the handbook.
- Change the cycle to Basic Bread.

Grain-Free Bread

Cooking Time: 45 Minutes
Servings: 2
Nutritional Analysis:

Calories: 163

Total Fat: 3g

Carbohydrates: 28g

Fiber: 1g

Ingredients:

- 2 cups of rice flour and potato starch
- half a cup of tapioca flour
- 1/2 tsp. xanthan gum
- 12 cup of non-dairy milk replacement or 2 and a half tablespoons of powdered milk 1.5 tablespoons of salt
- 1 1/2 teaspoons of egg replacer (optional) Sugar, 3 Tablespoons
- 2/3 cup of room temperature water
- 1 1/2 tbsp of dry yeast granules
- (4 tbsp) melted butter or margarine Just one teaspoon of vinegar

Instructions:

- Three eggs, room temperature
- Get out the bread pan and sprinkle it some yeast.
- Mix in the sugar, salt, milk powder, xanthan gum, and flours.
- Eggs, water, butter, and vinegar are beaten together and then added.
- To bake white bread, use the medium or 3-to 4-hour option.

Loaf With Olives And Cheddar

Cooking Time: 40 Minutes
Servings: 3
Nutritional Analysis:

Calories: 163

Total Fat: 4 g

Carbohydrates: 26g

Fiber: 1.6 g

Ingredients:

- 1-cup serving of room temperature water About 4 tsp. of sugar
- 1/4 teaspoon of salt
- together with 3 cups of bread flour, 1 1/2 cups of shredded strong cheddar cheese,
- a couple of tablespoons of dried active yeast
- pimiento olives, about a third of a cup, drained and sliced

Instructions:

- Put everything in the bread maker except the olive oil and follow the manufacturer's directions.
- Select Basic/White Bread and a Light crust setting on the bread maker. To begin, please press the "start" button.
- Let the bread machine do its thing and listen for the beep; that's when you'll know it's time to add the rest of the ingredients. The olives should be added now.
- There is still baking time left, so please be patient.
- When the bread machine beeps to indicate that it's done, remove the loaf's container and let it sit for five minutes.
- Shake the bucket to loosen the loaf, then lift it out and place it on a cooling rack.
- Have fun eating!

Mousse With Mozzarella And Salami

Cooking Time: 50 Minutes
Servings: 4
Nutritional Analysis:

Calories: 193

Total Fat: 3.0 g

Carbohydrates: 35g

Fiber: 3g

Ingredients:

- A quarter cup of water, heated to 80 degrees
- Shredded mozzarella cheese (about a third of a cup) Four tablespoons of sugar
- Two-thirds of a teaspoon of salt
- 13 tsp of dried basil Powdered garlic, about a pinch
- Increased to 2 cups 1 Tablespoon all-purpose flour Yeast, Instant, 1 Tablespoon
- 1/2 cup chopped hot salami

Instructions:

- Put everything in your bread machine except the salami and bake as directed.
- Select Basic/White Bread and a Light crust setting on the bread maker. To begin, please press the "start" button.
- Let the bread machine do its thing and listen for the beep; that's when you'll know it's time to add the rest of the ingredients. Mix in the salami now.
- There is still baking time left, so please be patient.
- When the bread machine beeps to indicate that it's done, remove the loaf's container and let it sit for five minutes.
- Shake the bucket to loosen the loaf, then lift it out and place it on a cooling rack.
- Have fun eating!

Anise Loaf, A Medium To Stab At

Cooking Time: 35 Minutes
Servings: 3
Nutritional Analysis:

Calories: 193

Total Fat: 6 g

Carbohydrates: 35g

Fiber: 3g

Ingredients:

- 3/4 cup water, at around 80 degrees Fahrenheit A single egg, at ambient temperature
- 2, and a half, thirds of a tablespoon of melted, cooled butter A little over 2 and a half teaspoons of honey
- 1/4 teaspoon pepper
- Anise Seed, About 2/3 Teaspoon 1/4 of a teaspoon of lemon juice Two Cups All-Purpose Flour
- 1.53 grams of instant yeast

Instructions:

- Follow the manufacturer's directions for your bread maker and add the ingredients mentioned.
- Select Basic/White Bread and a Light crust setting on the bread maker. To begin, please press the "start" button.
- There is still baking time left, so please be patient.
- When the bread machine beeps to indicate that it's done, remove the loaf's container and let it sit for five minutes.
- Shake the bucket to loosen the loaf, then lift it out and place it on a cooling rack.
- Have fun eating!

Tasty Honey Bread

Cooking Time: **35** Minutes
Servings: 3
Nutritional Analysis:

Calories: 193

Total Fat: 6 g

Carbohydrates: 35g

Fiber: 3g

Ingredients:

- 3/4 cup of room temperature milk Honey, about 2 teaspoons
- 1 tablespoon of melted, cooled butter
- 1/4 teaspoon of salt
- 1/4 cup all-purpose flour
- 1/2 cup smashed prepared granola 1 1/4 cups all-purpose flour
- Yeast for the bread maker, 1 teaspoon

Instructions:

- Follow the manufacturer's directions for your bread maker and add the ingredients mentioned.
- Select Basic/White Bread and a Medium crust setting on the bread maker. To begin, please press the "start" button.
- There is still baking time left, so please be patient.
- When the bread machine beeps to indicate that it's done, remove the loaf's container and let it sit for five minutes.
- Shake the bucket to loosen the loaf, then lift it out and place it on a cooling rack.
- Have fun eating!

Zucchini Herb Loaf

Cooking Time: 35 Minutes
Servings: 2
Nutritional Analysis:

Calories: 183

Total Fat: 3.28 g

Carbohydrates: 30g

Fiber: 4g

Ingredients:

- 1/3 of a liter of water
- honey, teaspoons
- 1/2 teaspoon salt
- 1/4 cup grated zucchini
- 1-and-a-quarter cups of 100% whole wheat flour 2 cups all-purpose flour
- 2 tablespoons of sesame seeds 1 tablespoon of minced fresh basil
- a single teaspoon of salt
- Active dry yeast equal to 1 1/2 teaspoons

Instructions:

- Follow the manufacturer's directions for your bread maker and add the ingredients mentioned.
- Select Basic/White Bread and a Medium crust setting on the bread maker. To begin, please press the "start" button.
- There is still baking time left, so please be patient.
- When the bread machine beeps to indicate that it's done, remove the loaf's container and let it sit for five minutes.
- Shake the bucket to loosen the loaf, then lift it out and place it on a cooling rack.
- Have fun eating!

Cinnamon And Cranberry Loaf Of Dreams

Cooking Time: 50 Minutes
Servings: 4
Nutritional Analysis:

Calories: 173

Total Fat: 3.28 g

Carbohydrates: 28 g

Fiber: 1.5 g

Ingredients:

- Half a cup of water
- a few teaspoons of melted butter 2-12 teaspoons of sugar
- 1/2 cup all-purpose flour 1/2 cup bread flour
- 2 1/4 tablespoons of dried yeast 1/2 cup fresh cranberries Cinnamon: 1 1/2 tablespoons

Instructions:

- Follow the manufacturer's directions for your bread machine by adding all of the ingredients (except the cranberries) to the pan.
- Select Basic/White Bread and a Light crust setting on the bread maker. To begin, please press the "start" button.
- Let the bread machine do its thing and listen for the beep; that's when you'll know it's time to add the rest of the ingredients. The cranberries should be added now.
- There is still baking time left, so please be patient.
- When the bread machine beeps to indicate that it's done, remove the loaf's container and let it sit for five minutes.
- Shake the bucket to loosen the loaf, then lift it out and place it on a cooling rack.
- Have fun eating!

Delicious Blue Cheese And Red Onion Appetizer

Cooking Time: 40 Minutes
Servings: 3
Nutritional Analysis:

Calories: 173

Total Fat: 3. g

Carbohydrates: 20.89 g

Fiber: 1.5 g

Ingredients:

- 80 degrees, 3/4 cup plus 1 tbsp water 1. complete egg
- a couple of tablespoons of melted butter, room temperature Two teaspoons of sugar and three tablespoons of powdered skim milk
- 1/2 tsp. salt
- A quarter of a cup of crumbled blue cheese Amount: 2 tablespoons dried onion flakes Two Cups All-Purpose Flour
- 2 Tablespoons instant mashed potato flakes
- 1/4 teaspoon of dried active yeast

Instructions:

- Follow the manufacturer's directions for your bread maker and add the ingredients mentioned.
- Select Basic/White Bread and a Light crust setting on the bread maker. To begin, please press the "start" button.
- There is still baking time left, so please be patient.
- When the bread machine beeps to indicate that it's done, remove the loaf's container and let it sit for five minutes.
- Shake the bucket to loosen the loaf, then lift it out and place it on a cooling rack.
- Have fun eating!

Fine Bread From Italy

Cooking Time: 30 Minutes
Servings: 2
Nutritional Analysis:

Calories: 169

Total Fat: 4 g

Carbohydrates: 28.6 g

Fiber: 1.1 g

Ingredients:

- 3 cups all-purpose flour, preferably unbleached 5 grams of brown sugar
- 1-and-a-half tablespoons of salt
- One and one-eighth cups of hot (about 45 degrees Celsius) water (or around 110 degrees Fahrenheit) 1,500 milliliters of olive oil
- 1 egg and 12 teaspoons of dried active yeast
- 1 teaspoon of salt
- a heaping spoonful of toasted sesame seeds 1.25 grams cornmeal

Instructions:

- Place all of the ingredients in the bread machine except the egg, 1 tablespoon of water, sesame seeds, and corn flour. Choose the dough setting.
- The batter may be used to make two loaves of bread. Spread cornmeal on a baking sheet that has been buttered. Place loaves on pan seam side down. Water the bread by brushing it on top. Let rise until double, approximately 50 minutes.
- Turn the oven temperature up to 375 degrees Fahrenheit.
- Spread egg wash on the bread. Add some sesame seeds for flavor. Cut four slits across the top of the log, each approximately a quarter of an inch deep. Put some boiling water in a pot and set it on the base of the stove. Toast the bread for 25 to 30 minutes. For crispier crust, bake bread in the afternoon and reheat it for 5 minutes just before serving.

An Impressive Oatmeal Loafs

Cooking Time: 40 Minutes
Servings: 3
Nutritional Analysis:

Calories: 113

Total Fat: 3.2g

Carbohydrates: 28.9 g

Fiber: 1.9 g

Ingredients:

- 80-degree water temperature, 3/4 cup
- 2 tbsp of melted butter, chilled 2 tbsp of sugar
- a single teaspoon of salt
- A quarter cup of instant oats
- One and a half cups all-purpose flour One teaspoon active dry yeast
- Follow the manufacturer's directions for your bread maker and add the ingredients mentioned.
- Select Basic/White Bread and a Light crust setting on the bread maker. To begin, please press the "start" button.
- There is still baking time left, so please be patient.
- When the bread machine beeps to indicate that it's done, remove the loaf's container and let it sit for five minutes.
- Shake the bucket to loosen the loaf, then lift it out and place it on a cooling rack.
- Have fun eating!
- The Baker's Secret to Better Bread from Your Bread Machine
- 7 ounces of hot (around 110 F/45 C) water. Lard, about 2 teaspoons
- 1-ounce container of active dry yeast 2 and 3/4 cups all-purpose flour
- a single teaspoon of salt
- Cinnamon, ground, one teaspoon (optional)

Instructions:

- The bread machine's instructions aren't necessary.
- Get some warm water and some fat and put them in the bread maker.
- Add yeast.
- The mixture needs salt and flour, so add them.
- Throw in some cinnamon if you like.
- Turn the machine on and choose the cycle setting.

Breads Made From Alligator Animals In Italian Style

Cooking Time: 50 Minutes
Servings: 2
Nutritional Analysis:

Calories: 156

Total Fat: 3g

Carbohydrates: 28 g

Fiber: 1.5 g

Ingredients:

- Hot water (around 110 degrees Fahrenheit, or 45 degrees Celsius) for one cup Three cups of flour, any kind
- measuring spoonful of active wheat gluten (optional) Salt, about 1 1/2 teaspoons
- 1/2 tsp. of dry yeast
- 2 grapes
- 1 egg
- cup of coffee or tea

Instructions:

- Put the water, flour, gluten (if using), salt, and yeast in the bread machine and let the dough cycle do the work. Good dough separation from the sides is a must. If the dough starts to become too dry or sticky, just add a little more water or flour during the mixing process. The first rising is complete when you punch the dough down and turn it out onto a floured board.
- Prepare a baking sheet with oil or parchment paper. Spread the dough into a 3/4-inch square and cut it into quarters. You'll need three total, so cut them out, jelly-roll style, and arrange them on a baking sheet, seam side down, to make a head, body, and tail. It's important to make sure the ends of the joined parts barely touch. (The dough will rise and the pieces will become larger, so try to maintain the sizes about the same.)
- Spread a thin layer of fat on your hands and collect the dough in your palms as you would clay. Thicken the tip of the nose and lengthen the tail to make a snout. Make an alligator's mouth by slicing horizontally through the tip of the snout; after the mouth is cut out, a wedge of greased aluminum foil may be used to keep it open.
- Reduce the leftover dough by a quarter and cut out two little circles for the eyes. Make four "logs" out of the remaining material to use as the legs. In order to install the alligator's legs, you must first flatten one end of each one and then slide it under its body. Then, before placing them on the baking sheet, gently bend the legs to make them more uniform in size. Create claws by slicing off little sections of the opposite leg. Use scissors to make shallow slits in the dough's top layer; these will serve as the alligator's spines. To make the eyes, roll the remaining dough into little balls and insert a raisin into each.
- Prepare an oven temperature of 200 degrees Celsius (400 degrees Fahrenheit). Combine the egg and the tablespoon of hot water in a small bowl and whisk until smooth.
- Alligator dough needs approximately half an hour to prove (press into the dough with your index and middle finger and the indentation should persist) in a warm place. If the dough bounces back, it needs more time to rise. To get the dough golden brown, brush it with the egg wash and bake it for 20 minutes in a preheated oven. Remove the alligator from the baking sheet using a spatula and set it up on a wire rack to cool. Remove the foil after it has cooled.

Chapter 10: Vegetable Bread Recipes
Traditional Amish Bread

Cooking Time: 50 Minutes
Servings: 4
Nutritional Analysis:

Calories: 163

Total Fat: 8 g

Carbohydrates: 40 g

Fiber: 5 g

Ingredients:

- Measurements: 3/4 cups bread flour 1/4 cup canola oil
- 1 tsp. of dried active yeast
- 1/4 cup white sugar
- 1/2 tsp. salt
- The equivalent of 18 tablespoons of hot water

Instructions:

- Put the ingredients in the bread machine pan in the sequence recommended by the manufacturer. Change the settings to the White Bread setting and start the machine.
- Once the dough has doubled in size and a second kneading cycle has begun, the machine should be turned off. For a do-over, start again by pressing the Start button. The procedure involves two complete rising cycles for the dough before the final rise before baking.

Simple White Bread

Cooking Time: 50 Minutes
Servings: 4
Nutritional Analysis:

Calories: 163

Total Fat: 8 g

Carbohydrates: 40 g

Fiber: 5 g

Ingredients:

- 1.25 cups of hot water
- 1 tablespoon of softened butter Approximately 1 tbsp of white sugar
- a single teaspoon of salt
- Bread flour equivalent to three cups
- Dry milk powder, 2 tbsp 1 packet of dried active yeast

Instructions:

- Put the ingredients in the pan of the bread machine in the sequence recommended by the manufacturer.
- To use the machine, choose "White Bread" from the menu and push "Start."

Bread With Sun-Dried Tomatoes And Basil

Cooking Time: 30 Minutes
Servings: 2
Nutritional Analysis:

Calories: 183

Total Fat: 3.6 g

Carbohydrates: 28 g

Fiber: 5g

Ingredients:

- 1/4 teaspoon dry active yeast 3 cups all-purpose flour
- a few Tablespoons of Wheat Bran 1/4 cup quinoa
- Dry milk powder, 3 teaspoons 1.5 grams fresh basil
- Sun-dried tomatoes, chopped, 1/4 cup a single teaspoon of salt
- 1/4 liter of water
- Cover with 1 cup of boiling water.

Instructions:

- Sun-dried tomato halves may be rehydrated by covering them with hot water in a small dish. Ten minutes of soaking time, then drain and bring to room temperature. Cut into pieces that are a quarter of an inch long.
- Put all of the ingredients into the bread machine pan in the sequence specified by the manufacturer. Press the button labeled "Start" after selecting the "Basic" or "White Bread" setting on the bread maker.

White Bread From BAXIS

Cooking Time: 45 Minutes
Servings: 2
Nutritional Analysis:

Calories: 163

Total Fat: 3.3 g

Carbohydrates: 28g

Fiber: 4 g

Ingredients:

- Active dry yeast equal to 1 1/2 teaspoons 2 cups all-purpose flour
- a single teaspoon of salt
- Approximately 1 tbsp of white sugar
- The equivalent of 1 teaspoon of dry milk powder 1 tablespoon of softened butter
- 34 cup water

Instructions:

- Ingredients should be added to the bread machine pan in the sequence recommended by the manufacturer.
- Then, choose the middle setting and hit the button labeled "Start."
- When the bread is done, remove it from the pan and set it on a cooling rack.
- The Finest Bread Ever Produced by a Bread Machine
- Hot water (around 110 degrees Fahrenheit, or 45 degrees Celsius) for one cup White sugar, 2 tablespoons
- Ingredients: 1 packet of bread machine yeast (.25 ounces)
- 1/2 cup of olive oil Bread flour equivalent to three cups a single teaspoon of salt
- Pour the water, sugar, and yeast into the bread machine's pan.
- Keep the yeast at room temperature for 10 minutes to let it dissolve and start foaming.
- The oil, wheat, and salt should be added now.
- To make white bread or basic bread, choose the appropriate option and click the Start button.
- Bread made with buttermilk and white flour
- 1 & 1/8 ounces
- Honey, 3 Tablespoons' Worth
- One Tablespoon of Margarine One and a Half Tablespoons of Salt
- Bread flour equivalent to three cups
- 2-tablespoons of dried active yeast
- Buttermilk powder, measuring out 4 teaspoons

Instructions:

- To use a bread machine, put the ingredients in the pan in the order recommended by the manufacturer. To make white bread and a medium crust, choose those options.
- In the hot and sticky summer, less yeast is needed.

Make Cinnamon Swirl Bread In The Bread Machine

Cooking Time: 40 Minutes
Servings: 3
Nutritional Analysis:

Calories: 13

Total Fat: 3 g

Carbohydrates: 28 g

Fiber: 1.11 g

Ingredients:

- 1 glass milk
- eggs
- 14 cup butter
- 4 cups all-purpose flour
- 1/4 cup white sugar a single teaspoon of salt
- 1/2 tsp. of dried active yeast
- 1/2 a cup of chopped walnuts
- 12 tins of brown sugar
- two to three tablespoons of cinnamon powder
- butter, softened to a tablespoon and a half, divided
- Confectioner's sugar, 2 teaspoons' worth, sifted (optional)

Instructions:

- Add the milk, eggs, 1/4 cup butter, bread flour, sugar, salt, and yeast to the bread machine in the order specified by the manufacturer; choose the Dough setting; and press the Start button. After the machine has completed its cycle, transfer the dough to a floured work area and punch it down to release air bubbles. You should give the dough a rest for 10 minutes.
- Stir together the ground cinnamon, chopped walnuts, and brown sugar in a bowl.
- The dough should be cut in half and rolled out into 14-by-9-inch rectangles. Spread 1 tablespoon of softened butter over the surface of the dough, then sprinkle half of the walnut mixture over the butter. Fill the rectangles of dough, then roll them up from the shorter ends and seal the seams by pinching them together.
- Prepare two 9-by-5-inch loaf pans by coating them with oil. Put the filled loaves, seam side down, into the prepared loaf pans. Allow the dough to rise in a covered bowl until it has about doubled in size, approximately 30 minutes.
- Turn the oven temperature up to 350 degrees Fahrenheit (175 degrees Celsius).
- Bake the dough for 30 minutes in a preheated oven, or until it is a light golden brown and makes a hollow sound when you tap the bottom of the loaf. Cover the loaves loosely with aluminum foil for the last 10 minutes of baking if they begin to brown too quickly. Bread should cool for 10 minutes in the pan before being transferred to wire racks to cool entirely. Sprinkle 1 teaspoon of confectioners' sugar over the top of each loaf.

Traditional White Bread

Cooking Time: 40 Minutes
Servings: 3
Nutritional Analysis:

Calories: 153

Total Fat: 3.1 g

Carbohydrates: 28.9 g

Fiber: 1.15 g

Ingredients:

- 1.25 ounces of hot (or boiling, at 110 degrees Fahrenheit/45 degrees Celsius) water. White sugar, 3 tablespoons
- 1-and-a-half tablespoons of salt
- Three Tablespoons of Oil from a Vegetable Source Bread flour equivalent to three cups
- 2 and 14 tablespoons of dry yeast

Instructions:

- Combine the yeast, bread flour, sugar, water, oil, salt, and bread machine pan.
- Put the oven to the White Bread setting. Make sure to let things cool completely on wire racks before cutting into them.

Super Light, White Bread

Cooking Time: 40 Minutes
Servings: 3
Nutritional Analysis:

Calories: 173

Total Fat: 3.9 g

Carbohydrates: 28 g

Fiber: 3 g

Ingredients:

- 1 mug of hot water 2 Tablespoons of White Sugar
- 3.25 cups bread flour 2.25 teaspoons yeast
- 14 cup of melted butter 14 teaspoon of salt

Instructions:

- Put the yeast, sugar, and 2 tablespoons of the warm water (save the other 4 tablespoons for later) into the bread machine. Provide a mixture that can be quickly dissolved. Ten minutes at most should be allowed for the mixture to become frothy and effervescent.

- Start the tangoing with 3 tablespoons of flour and 2 tablespoons of water in a saucepan over low heat until a beautiful gooey roux is produced while your yeast starts going. About two minutes is all that's needed for this.
- Add the Tangoing starter, butter, salt, and flour to your bread machine (in that sequence).
- Start the bread maker with the "dough" and let it alone.
- After the dough cycle is complete, transfer the dough to a floured board, divide it in two, and punch it.
- The dough should be divided evenly between two loaf pans.
- As the batter is being risen for a second time, preheat the oven to 350 degrees.
- Fill an oven-safe jar with about 2 cups of water and put it in the oven. There wouldn't be a tough, hard crust since the water would emit steam.
- As soon as the oven is preheated, place the loaf pans inside and bake for 30 minutes.
- Bread should be kept in a plastic bag with a zip top for about a week to keep it soft and fresh.
- finished processing and suitable for consumption.

Dough Worked With Banana

Cooking Time: 28 Minutes
Servings: 3
Nutritional Analysis:

Calories: 170

Total Fat: 3g

Carbohydrates: 28g

Fiber: 1g

Ingredients:

- baking powder, 1 teaspoon A pinch of baking soda
- Peel and cut bananas in half lengthwise 2 cups all-purpose flour
- eggs
- vegetable oil 1 tbsp A little less than a half a cup of white sugar

Instructions:

- Combine everything in the bread pan, and bake using the dough setting. Start mixing for three to five minutes.
- Press the stop button after three to five minutes. Please stop combining. Bring the dough's surface to a smooth consistency.
- Select bake, hit start, and let it cook for roughly 50 minutes, all while using the spatula. When the 50 minutes are up, poke it in the middle of the top with a toothpick to see if it's done.
- Do another taste test on the bread. At the end of the baking time, take the pan out of the oven but leave the bread inside for another 10 minutes. Take out the bread and let it cool on a rack.

Traditional Bread With Oranges And Nuts

Cooking Time: 50 Minutes
Servings: 4
Nutritional Analysis:

Calories: 166

Total Fat: 3.0 g

Carbohydrates: 28g

Fiber: 3 g

Ingredients:

- An Egg White, Measured Out
- 1 teaspoon of salt
- yeast, 1 tablespoon, and half a cup of warm whey
- About 4 tbsp of sugar
- Two oranges, smashed
- Quantity of Flour Needed: 4 Cups
- a single teaspoon of salt
- 1 & 1/2 teaspoons of salt orange peel, 3 tablespoons Half a grain of vanilla
- Crushed walnuts and almonds, 3 teaspoons Season with crushed pepper, salt, and grated cheese.

Instructions:

- Add everything to the bread machine except the egg white, tablespoon of water, and crushed pepper/cheese.
- Put the machine through its "Dough" cycle.
- Carefully transfer the dough to a floured work surface (using floured hands to do so).
- The dough has to rise for 10 minutes after being covered with a thin film of cling paper.
- After letting the dough rise, cut it into thirds.
- Roll out each half on a floured surface into 14-by-10-inch rectangles.
- Cut the dough into 1/2-inch-wide strips using a sharp knife.
- Select a few of strips and twist them several times, pressing the ends together after each twist.
- Bake at 400 degrees Fahrenheit.
- To make the egg wash, combine the egg white and water in a dish.
- Season with salt and pepper or cheese.
- Put in the oven for 10 to 12 minutes, or until browned.
- Take out of the oven and place on a cooling rack. Support and
- enjoy!

Cinnamon And Apple Bread

Cooking Time: 40 Minutes
Servings: 3
Nutritional Analysis:

Calories: 170

Total Fat: 3.0 g

Carbohydrates: 28 g

Fiber: 1.3 g

Ingredients:

- Apples, dry, diced; 1/3 cup; bread machine yeast; 1/2 tsp 4 cups all-purpose flour
- a quarter of a cup of chopped pecans
- Mix in a pinch of ground nutmeg, little more than a quarter teaspoon Only a pinch of ground ginger Add 1/4 teaspoon ground allspice
- Mix together 1/2 tsp. ground cinnamon and 1 1/4 tsp. salt
- butter, unsalted, cubed tablespoons dry skim milk powder, 1/3 cup
- A Quarter Cup of Honey
- At room temperature, crack open 2 jumbo eggs. Half a cup of canned pumpkin puree

Instructions:

- Approximately 2/3 cup of water, between 80- and 90-degrees Fahrenheit (26 and 32 degrees Celsius)
- Except for the dried apples, add the following to the bread pan: water, pumpkin puree, eggs, honey, skim milk, butter, salt, allspice, cinnamon, nuts, nutmeg, ginger, flour, and yeast.
- Put the dish in the dishwasher and close the lid.
- You should put the dried apples in the nut and fruit dispenser.
- Activate the device. Pick the sugary mode and the crust hue you like.
- Once the bread has cooked, carefully remove it from the mold and let it cool for at least 20 minutes before cutting it.

Bread With Butter Cream And Peaches

Cooking Time: 40 Minutes
Servings: 3
Nutritional Analysis:

Calories: 153

Total Fat: 3.6g

Carbohydrates: 28g

Fiber: 3g

Ingredients:

- Cut up and drain 3/4 cup of canned peaches 1/3 cup of cold thick whipping cream Single egg, room temperature
- 2 and a quarter teaspoons of sugar 1 tablespoon of melted butter
- salt - 1/8 teaspoon
- Just a third of a teaspoon of ground cinnamon Nutmeg, ground: 1/8 teaspoon one-third of a cup of whole wheat flour
- 3/4 cup all-purpose flour
- Instant or bread machine yeast, equivalent to 1 16 tablespoons

Instructions:

- Get the ingredients ready. Make use of your Hamilton Beach bread maker by placing the ingredients there.
- Put the oven onto bake mode. To make Whitbread, just enter the appropriate instructions, choose either a light or medium crust, and tap Start.
- Take the bucket out of the machine after the bread is done.
- It's best to wait 5 minutes before cutting into the bread.
- Remove the loaf by shaking the container, then set it on a cooling rack.

Pumpernickel Bread With Cinnamon And Sugared Raisins

Cooking Time: 40 Minutes
Servings: 3
Nutritional Analysis:

Calories: 153

Total Fat: 3.6g

Carbohydrates: 28g

Fiber: 3g

Ingredients:

- cup Flour for Bread 13 cup of rye flour 3/4 cup of wheat flour
- Half a cup of room temperature water
- measure out 2 teaspoons of cocoa powder
- Oil or shortening, melted, 6 tablespoons Salinity, Half a Tablespoon
- Yeast, instant, 1 tablespoon A Half Cup of Molasses
- A Quarter Cup of Honey
- Half a Tablespoon of Cinnamon Roughly 1 cup of raisins

Instructions:

- Get the ingredients ready. Put the water, molasses, salt, and oil into a bowl and mix well. Mix together completely by stirring.
- Aside from the raisins, combine all of the ingredients in the bread pan in the order of liquid-dry yeast.
- Close the lid of the Hamilton Beach bread maker and place the pan inside.
- Put the raisins into the vending machine.
- Put the oven onto bake mode. Use a loaf made using whole wheat flour.
- Turn the switch to "on" and wait for the bread to finish baking.
- Once the bread is finished baking, the machine will switch to a keep warm setting.
- Leave it plugged in for around 10 minutes after you've set it to that setting.
- Take the pan away and let it sit for approximately ten minutes to cool down.

A Loaf Of Zucchini And Berries

Cooking Time: 30 Minutes
Servings: 2
Nutritional Analysis:

Calories: 133

Total Fat: 2 g

Carbohydrates: 25 g

Fiber: 3 g

Ingredients:

- One-fourth cup of flour
- A little whisking of eggs. 1.5 ounces of sugar
- Vanilla extract, 2 tablespoons; vegetable oil, 3/4 cup
- Powdered sugar, half a cup baking soda, just a pinch
- 1/2-gram salt
- A measure of cinnamon equal to 2 teaspoons Half a cup of blueberries
- one and a half cups of shredded zucchini
- Get the ingredients ready. Separately combine the dry and wet components.

Instructions:

- All of the components (save the berries) should be layered in the bread pan as follows: liquid, dry yeast, zucchini.
- Close the lid of the Hamilton Beach bread maker and place the pan inside.
- Put the berry jars into the machine that dispenses them.
- Put the oven onto bake mode. Put in the oven and bake for 1 hour on High White Speed. To begin, please press the "start" button.
- Put the berries in at the five-minute mark of the cycle.
- Let the bread bake for a while.
- Once the bread is finished baking, the machine will switch to a keep warm setting.
- Leave it plugged in for 10 minutes after switching modes.
- Take the pan away and let it sit for approximately ten minutes to cool down.

Carrot Bread With Yeast

Cooking Time: 30 Minutes
Servings: 2
Nutritional Analysis:

Calories: 133

Total Fat: 2 g

Carbohydrates: 25 g

Fiber: 3 g

Ingredients:

- Milk, 3/4 cup
- Ingredients: 1 tablespoon honey 3 tablespoons of melted butter
- A little over a cup and a half of shredded carrot
- 14 tsp. of nutmeg powder
- 1/2 tsp. salt
- Three cups of all-purpose flour
- Yeast, dry, 2 and a quarter teaspoon

Instructions:

- Get the ingredients ready. Make use of your Hamilton Beach bread maker by placing the ingredients there.
- Put the oven onto bake mode. Quick bread should be selected and the machine started.
- Take the bucket out of the machine once the bread is done.
- It's best to wait 5 minutes before cutting into the bread.
- The loaf may be removed from the bucket by gently shaking it and then placed on a cooling rack.

Rolls Of Mixed Berries

Cooking Time: 40 Minutes
Servings: 3
Nutritional Analysis:

Calories: 133

Total Fat: 2 g

Carbohydrates: 25 g

Fiber: 3 g

Ingredients:

- 4 cups all-purpose flour
- 14 cups of brown sugar
- Cut in half a cup, one-third of a cup of dried cherries Chopped dried blueberries (about a third of a cup) Yeast (about 2 tablespoons)
- 1.25 grams of salt
- container for liquid (cup)
- a few Tablespoons of Oil from a Vegetable Source

Instructions:

- Sprinkle the dry ingredients over the wet ones after pouring the water and oil into the bread pan.
- To use the bread machine, choose the "Normal" or "Basic" setting.
- Select a crust setting of either light or medium brown.
- Remove the bread from the cycles and place it on a wire rack to cool.
- Before slicing, allow the bread to cool fully.
- Toasted Rye Bread with Zucchini
- Flour, either all-purpose or bread flour, to the measure of 2 cups Roughly 2 3/4 cups of rye flour
- A measure of cocoa powder equal to 2 teaspoons 1/4 cup flour
- Yeast, instant, 1 tablespoon 14 cup of olive oil
- Equal parts honey or molasses, about 3 teaspoons A cup and a half of room temperature water
- a single teaspoon of salt
- Shredded Zucchini equivalent to 1 1/2 cups
- Get the ingredients ready. Shredded zucchini should be dried by wringing it out with a towel to eliminate extra moisture.
- Layer the liquid, zucchini, flour, and yeast in a container.
- Close the lid of the Hamilton Beach bread maker and place the pan inside.
- Put the oven onto bake mode. Pick white bread with a somewhat thick crust.
- Turn the switch to "on" and wait for the bread to finish baking.
- Once the bread is finished baking, the machine will switch to a keep warm setting.
- Leave it plugged in for roughly 10 minutes after switching it to that mode.
- Take the pan away and let it rest for approximately ten minutes to cool.

Crunchy Onion Bread

Cooking Time: 40 Minutes
Servings: 4
Nutritional Analysis:

Calories: 180

Total Fat: 5g

Carbohydrates: 30g

Fiber: 5g

Ingredients:

- 80°F to 90°F, 1 cup of water
- 1 1/2 teaspoons of sugar 3 tablespoons of melted butter
- The equivalent of eleven and an eighth teaspoons of salt
- Amount: 3 tablespoons dry minced onion
- fresh chives, chopped (1 and a half teaspoons) Three cups of all-purpose flour
- 1/2 a packet of active dry yeast or 1 teaspoon of bread machine yeast

Instructions:

- Get the ingredients ready. Make use of your Hamilton Beach bread maker by placing the ingredients there.
- Put the oven onto bake mode. Set the bread maker to make Whitbread, choose a thin or regular crust, then push Start.
- Take the bucket out of the equipment.
- It's best to wait 5 minutes before cutting into the bread.
- Shake the bucket carefully and place it on a cooling rack.

Cream Bread And Peaches

Cooking Time: 40 Minutes
Servings: 4
Nutritional Analysis:

Calories: 163

Total Fat: 3 g

Carbohydrates: 28 g

Fiber: 1g

Ingredients:

- a half cup of peaches from a can, chopped
- 1/4 cup of chilled heavy cream, between 80- and 90-degrees Single egg, room temperature
- The equivalent of 1 1/2 teaspoons of sugar, plus 3/4 of a tablespoon of melted butter
- Salinity, 3/4 teaspoon
- 1/4 tsp. of cinnamon powder Nutmeg, ground: 1/8 teaspoon
- Whole wheat flour, 1/4 cup
- 1 3/4 ounces all-purpose flour
- 3/4 teaspoons rapid or bread machine yeast

Instructions:

- Put everything in the bread maker according to the instructions.
- Put the ingredients in, choose the crust setting that will yield a medium loaf of Basic White bread, and push Start.
- Take the bucket away from the bread maker after the loaf is done baking.
- Relax for five minutes as it cools off.
- Remove the loaf from the bucket by shaking it gently, and place it on a cooling rack.

Spicy Warm Pumpkin Bread

Cooking Time: 45 Minutes
Servings: 3
Nutritional Analysis:

Calories: 150

Total Fat: 3.0g

Carbohydrates: 28 g

Fiber: 1.1 g

Ingredients:

- Butter to lubricate the jug Pureed pumpkin to the tune of 112 cups
- Three eggs, room temperature One-third cup of sugar, melted butter, and 1 cup of salt.
- Three cups of flour, any kind
- 2 tablespoons of flour
- a quarter of a teaspoon of cinnamon powder
- baking soda, half a teaspoon
- 14 tsp of ground nutmeg
- a pinch of dried ginger
- a pinch of ground cloves and salt
- Spread some softened butter in the bread basket.
- Put the pumpkin in a bowl and add the eggs, butter, and sugar.

Instructions:

- To use the machine quickly, set the controls to the Quick/Rapid mode and hit the Start button.
- When the initial rapid mixing cycle is complete, after roughly 10 minutes, the paddles may continue incorporating the wet components.
- Follow the instructions and give it a good stir. Toss together the flour, baking powder, cinnamon, baking soda, nutmeg, ginger, salt, and cloves until everything is well distributed.
- When the second quick mixing cycle begins, add the dry ingredients to the bucket.
- Take the bucket away from the bread maker after the loaf is done baking.
- Place the bread in the refrigerator for five minutes to cool.
- Remove the loaf from the bucket and place it on a cooling rack.

Bread With Mushrooms And Leeks

Cooking Time: 45 Minutes
Servings: 3
Nutritional Analysis:

Calories: 150

Total Fat: 3.0g

Carbohydrates: 28 g

Fiber: 1.1 g

Ingredients:

- The equivalent of 2 tablespoons of butter
- The equivalent of 2 cups of chopped mushrooms Favored Portobello Mushrooms 1/4 of an onion, diced
- An ounce and a half of dried thyme A cup and a third of water
- Salt, 1/2 teaspoon
- honey, by the tablespoonful, in liquid form
- 34 cup all-purpose flour
- 3/3.5 cups bread flour or all-purpose flour One teaspoon of bread machine yeast

Instructions:

- Begin by melting butter over medium heat in a pot. Sauté the mushrooms, leeks, and thyme until they are soft. Put it in a baking dish right away.
- The other ingredients should be measured out and placed in the baking dish in the sequence suggested by the maker. Put the pan in the oven.
- Please choose Basic Cycle.

Strictly Peached Bread

Cooking Time: 40 Minutes
Servings: 3
Nutritional Analysis:

Calories: 160

Total Fat: 3.8 g

Carbohydrates: 28g

Fiber: 5g

Ingredients:

- Peaches (about a third of a cup): chopped
- One-third of a cup of cream used for whipping 1 egg
- 1 Tablespoon of softened butter, room temperature Just a third of a teaspoon of ground cinnamon
- Nutmeg, ground: 1/8 teaspoon 2 1/4 teaspoons of sugar
- 1.182 grams of salt
- one-third of a cup of whole wheat flour the equivalent of two and a half cups of all-purpose flour
- 1/2 cup flour 1/8 teaspoon active dry yeast
- To a loaf pan that holds 1 1/2 pounds of food, first add the liquid components, and then the dry ingredients.

Instructions:

- Put the prepared loaf pan into the bread maker and secure the cover.
- Press "Basic Bread," "White Bread," or "Regular Bread" to pick a bread cycle, and then press "Light" or "Medium" for the crust setting.
- Turn on the machine, and it will immediately begin making the bread.
- When the bread loaf is done, remove the loaf pan by lifting the lid.
- Give the pan ten to fifteen minutes to cool on a wire rack. Remove the bread loaf from the pan and give it a little shake.
- Create slices and serve.

Bread With Date Delight

Cooking Time: 35 Minutes
Servings: 3
Nutritional Analysis:

Calories: 153

Total Fat: 3g

Carbohydrates: 28 g

Fiber: 1.5 g

Ingredients:

- Quarter of a cup of room temperature water
- a half cup of room temperature milk
- four tablespoons of butter, softened to room temperature
- 1/3 tsp. vanilla extract
- two table spoons of molasses
- a sugar measure equivalent to a tablespoon
- 1/2 cup all-purpose flour 1/4 cup whole-wheat flour 1 1/4 cups all-purpose flour
- Two Tablespoons of Nonfat Dry Milk a single teaspoon of salt
- 2/3 cup sugar 1 tablespoon cocoa powder
- 1/2 tsp of dry yeast, rapid rise, or bread machine yeast Dates, about 3/4 cup chopped

Instructions:

- To a loaf pan that holds 1 1/2 pounds of food, first add the liquid components, and then the dry ingredients. (As of right now, don't include the dates.)
- Put the prepared loaf pan into the bread maker and secure the cover.
- Connect the bread maker to an electrical outlet. To pick a bread cycle, press "Basic Bread," "White Bread," "Regular Bread," or "Fruit/Nut Bread," and then select a crust type by pressing "Light" or "Medium."
- Turn on the machine, and it will immediately begin making the bread. Add the dates when the computer prompts you to do so.
- When the bread loaf is done, remove the loaf pan by lifting the lid.
- Give the pan ten to fifteen minutes to cool on a wire rack. Remove the bread loaf from the pan and give it a little shake.
- Create slices and serve.

Spotted Vegetable Bread

Cooking Time: Minutes
Servings: 4
Nutritional Analysis:

Calories: 173

Total Fat: 3.28 g

Carbohydrates: 28.89 g

Fiber: 1.1 g

Ingredients:

- tablespoons (50 mL) buttermilk
- two and a half cups (250 grams) of whole wheat flour
- Panarin, 2 tablespoons
- Ingredients: 2 tsp yeast 1 1/2 tsp salt 1.5 grams of sugar
- Dry paprika, one tablespoon 2 teaspoons of beet powder
- 1.5 fresh cloves of garlic Two and a half cups' worth
- oil from vegetables, 1 tbsp

Instructions:

- Prepare baking timer for 4 hours; medium-brown crust is desired.
- Observe the dough-kneading procedure if you want perfectly smooth and fluffy buns.

Breakfast Bread With Tomatoes And Onions

Cooking Time: 45 Minutes
Servings: 2
Nutritional Analysis:

Calories: 190

Total Fat: 3.0g

Carbohydrates: 30 g

Fiber: 1.1 g

Ingredients:

- cups flour for all purposes 1/2 cup all-purpose flour
- 1/2 mug of hot water
- 140 milliliters, or 4 3/4 ounces, of milk. Three Tablespoons of Extra Virgin Olive Oil
- 1 cup of sugar
- pinch of salt
- tablespoons of instant yeast
- 1/4 teaspoon baking soda Five tomatoes dried in the sun
- 1 onion

Instructions:

- black pepper, to taste, 1/4 teaspoon
- Gather up everything that will be required. To sauté the onion, just cut it finely and add it to a skillet. Prepare the sun-dried tomatoes by chopping them (10 halves).
- Tomatoes and onions should be added to the bowl after the liquid components have been poured in. Add the yeast and baking powder to the liquid without stirring it.
- To begin baking, choose your mode. The bread machine may be set to knead the dough at moderate rates if you choose the Bread with Additives setting.

Chapter 11: Cheese Bread Recipes
Bread With Tomatoes

Cooking Time: 50 Minutes
Servings: 2
Nutritional Analysis:

Calories: 153

Total Fat: 3.28 g

Carbohydrates: 28.89 g

Fiber: 1.6 g

Ingredients:

- cup of tomato sauce 1.5 ounces (340 ml) of water
- 13 cup flour (560 grams)
- Eleven-and-a-half drops of oil from a vegetable source Add 2 tsp. of sugar
- Salt, to taste, 2 tablespoons
- 1 1/2 tablespoons of active dry yeast
- 1/2 tsp. dried oregano
- 1/2 tsp. ground sweet paprika

Instructions:

- Warm some water and dilute the tomato paste with it. To lessen the tomato taste, use less tomato paste, but using less than 1 tablespoon is pointless since the color will fade.
- Get the seasonings ready. For extra flavor, I upped the amount of oregano and paprika and also added some Provencal herbs (this bread also begs for spices).
- The flour will benefit from the added oxygen after being sieved. Flour + spices = deliciousness.
- Put the vegetable oil in the container of the bread machine. Combine the tomato puree, water, sugar, salt, spiced flour, and yeast.
- Kick on the bread machine (the Basic program – I have the White Bread – the crust Medium).
- Please remember to switch off the bread machine after the baking cycle is complete. Take out the bread and enjoy it fresh and hot. Cool it down for an hour on the grill.

Sour Bread Loaded With Eggs And Butter

Cooking Time: 50 Minutes
Servings: 2
Nutritional Analysis:

Calories: 150

Total Fat: 3.5 g

Carbohydrates: 28 g

Fiber: 1.6 g

Ingredients:

- two cups of cold water a quarter cup of cream
- a pair of eggs
- two teaspoons of salt
- 1 pound (three cups) of sourdough starter
- flour, and then some
- 2 1/4 teaspoons of dried active yeast
- salt, kosher, 1 tsp.
- Eight tablespoons of softened, unsalted butter
- Nonstandard cooking spray

Instructions:

- Put all the ingredients for the dough (flour, yeast, water, heavy cream, eggs, and sugar) into a stand mixer and mix on Add all ingredients to a mixer with a paddle and beat on medium speed for about five minutes, or until the batter is smooth.
- Sprinkle in the salt by the spoonful and work the mixture until the margarine is completely unified. Wrap the bowl in plastic and set it in a warm place for an hour to allow the Mixture rise and expand. While waiting, preheat a 9-by-5-inch amount skillet with a splash of water over medium heat. Pat the batter into an 8-by-8-inch square on a surface that has been lightly floured. To get the Mixture's focus point, place it over the overlap and push straight down on the edge.
- Reduce the height once again; this time, get to within an inch or so of these baselines. Seal the edge by pressing down. Now, close the crease you produced by pulling the bottom portion of the batter up to meet the mixture roll you've made. Closures zipped, drop batter into ready baking dish, crease side down.
- Wrap the skillet in plastic wrap or place the whole dish in a large plastic bag and secure the open end with a knot. Chill in the fridge for at least an hour and up to 24 hours before reheating. A longer period of rest is beneficial to the Mixture, but it should have grown to its full potential after around 6 hours.

Walter Sourdough Voiced

Cooking Time: 40 Minutes
Servings: 2
Nutritional Analysis:

Calories: 163

Total Fat: 4.5 g

Carbohydrates: 30g

Fiber: 1.81 g

Ingredients:

- the equivalent of 12.2 ounces / 345.9 grams of whole spelt flour in three half-cup measures
- 20 ounces (567 grams) of water equals two and a half cups' worth.
- a beginning of either Deem or Whole Wheat, one cup
- 8.4 ounces/238 grams of whole wheat flour (two cups' worth)
- one teaspoon (or.2 ounces/5.7 g) of salt.

Instructions:

- Put the ingredients through a medium-speed blender and blend until they are completely combined. About two minutes is the average time needed. After 20 minutes, let the mixture autolyze (rest). Once autolysis is complete, the batter should be consolidated for about 4 minutes at low speed. Then, after adding the essential ascent, let the combination massage for three to four hours until it has multiplied. After kneading, drop the dough by spoonful onto a lightly dusted (Spelt flour) surface and knead again, or twice, until a ball forms.
- Split the Mixture in half or a third. Shockingly, the quantities formed just 30 minutes apart. Form ingredients into the final form you want, and then let the batter 10 minutes to rest (seat rest). After the portions have rested, shape them back into their original forms and place them in a sealing skillet or bushels, lining them with sealing fabrics if desired (bannetons aren't have to be lined). It is okay to let the Mixture rise until the sealing is complete. The second rise in the mixture is the sealing. One and a half to two hours is a possible time range for the Its formula. Mixture is ready when it has a bubbly, springy, not drooping texture; at this time, take the main portion, sprinkle the top (really the underside) with semolina or whole grain flour, and turn the batter out onto a strip of flat prepared sheet. Then, you'll want to cut the batter while it's still on the strip, slip it onto a hot preparation stone in an oven prepared to 450 degrees Fahrenheit (232 degrees Celsius), quickly spritz the Mixture with water, and cover it with a cooking top. Cook for twenty minutes at high heat.
- After 20 minutes, start the stovetop and reduce the broiler temperature to 425F/218C. Sauté for another 15–20 minutes, rotating the quantity once. In order to prepare the resultant quantity, turn the heat back on and replace the simmering top; this will take around five minutes. Get ready with a sum that is secondary to the major one. Enjoy some late-night deliciousness by chilling out some savory bread and spreading it with some margarine. The sourdough version of spelt bread has a chewy shell and a tender, mushy crumb; it's great for sandwiches, toast, or eating straight up with some cream cheese.

Saturated To The Max Sourdough

Cooking Time: 45 Minutes
Servings: 1
Nutritional Analysis:

Calories: 155

Total Fat: 3.6 g

Carbohydrates: 28.78 g

Fiber: 3.1 g

Ingredients:

- Rye Flour, 1/2 Cup
- Two-and-a-half-thirds of a cup of whole wheat flour.
- Approximately One Ounce
- Six and a quarter cup
- 2 cups of a healthy sourdough starter
- Tender water, one cup's worth, in temperature
- a single teaspoon of oil
- a single measuring teaspoon of diastatic malt powder
- 3 grams of salt

Instructions:

- Combine the ingredients for at least two minutes, preferably three. Allow the Mixture to autolyze (rest) for 20 minutes. When the autolysis process is complete, add the salt and stir the mixture for about a minute at a low pace. Afterward, let the combination massage (which suggests that the essential ascent) for six to eight hours in a warm 80F/26.7C place.
- During the 6-to-8-hour massage process, fold the batter in a collapsible box or mix it down with just three spins of the mixing snare. The purpose is to strengthen the gluten, align the strands, and prevent the batter from staleness. When the bulk is ready, pour it out onto a floured surface and roll it around twice, or whatever many times are necessary, until it forms a ball.
- Arrange ingredients in the rough shape you require, and then let the batter rest for five to ten minutes (seat rest). After sidelining, form the quantities into their final bodies, then place them in sealing bushels or containers lined with sealing fabrics (Bannetons are not need to be lined). Let the batter rest at room temperature for 30 minutes before storing it in the fridge for a few hours, covered.
- If the Mixture has been active throughout the day, you won't need to wait the half hour. Next morning, remove the quantities 30 minutes apart (so you don't have to cook them at the same time). Next, let the batter to rise until the seal is complete. In the course of one to three hours, the volume of the mixture will have increased by around half. When the dough is ready and feels light and springy but not slack, scoop out the required quantity, dust the top (the bottom, technically) with semolina or whole grain flour, and turn out onto a strip of flat heating sheet.
- When ready to cook, cut the Mixture while it is still on the strip, place the batter on a hot heating stone in a fresh, warmed oven set to 450F/232.2C, quickly sprinkle it with water once, and then cover it with a cooking cover that has also been preheated in the oven. For 20 minutes, heat.

Neat As A Pin In The Style Of Berlin

Cooking Time: 45 Minutes
Servings: 2
Nutritional Analysis:

Calories: 150

Total Fat: 3.5 g

Carbohydrates: 28.89 g

Fiber: 1.7 g

Ingredients:

- one and a quarter cups of ripe, active starter one quarter cup of whole wheat flour
- 12 ounces is equal to half a cup.
- 13.5 ounces (about three cups) of bread flour

Instructions:

- Mix autolysis with salt and combine all ingredients until uniform. It may take around two or three minutes. Give the ingredients a rest for 20 minutes. Turn your Mixer back to its slowest setting once again, and let the ingredients meld for another two minutes. Tackiness is a possible result of the blend. Replace the variety in the aging chamber and collapse batter once day till 9:00 p.m. Next, you should temporarily store the holder in the refrigerator.
- Wrapping or sealing an item in plastic wrap or storing it in an airtight container might prevent it from drying out. After thirty minutes, you may begin to form the next sum. It should take two to three hours, or until the total seems around half its distinctive size, for the two quantities to warm up and conduct their last confirmation. When there is still an hour before you need to start heating, turn on your broiler and set the temperature to 450F/232.2C.
- Take the measured quantity, sprinkle the top (actually, the bottom) with semolina, and turn the batter out onto a strip of level prepared sheet when the mixture is organized and feels bouncy and springy to the touch. Next, you'll need to cut the batter while it's still on the strip, slide it onto a hot heating stone in an oven warmed to 450F/232.2C, quickly sprinkle the batter with water, and then cover it with a broiling top. Please devote about twenty minutes for prepping. In 20 minutes, remove the lid from the oven and reduce the heat under the broiler to 425 degrees Fahrenheit or 218 degrees Celsius. Searing will be achieved by continuing to heat for another 15 minutes and flipping the quantity once. Using a bread thermometer, check the center of the quantity to make sure it has reached 200 205F/93 96C.
- To prepare the corresponding quantity, re-cover the cooking broiler and warm it to 450F/232.2C. Get ready to use the same as your main figure. Its bread is at its harshest after being let to cool for a few hours. You'll continue to notice the sharp odor far into the next day.

Sour Dough Malt Bread

Cooking Time: 30 Minutes
Servings: 2
Nutritional Analysis:

Calories: 183

Total Fat: 5.28 g

Carbohydrates: 31.89 g

Fiber: 1.6 g

Ingredients:

- flour for baking bread; 1 lb. 13.5 oz.
- Mix in two tablespoons of malt syrup once the dough has finished rising.
- Starter for sourdough bread, 1 cup
- 40 ml (2 tbsp) or 20 oz.
- After the dough has had time to ferment, add the salt, which amounts to three teaspoons.
- 6 Ounce

Instructions:

- Make sure to save 6 ounces of the water, then the malt syrup, and finally the salt. This is so you may choose to use the Double Hydration Method, which you will learn about in the next section (Advanced). Mix all ingredients (except the 6 ounces of water, the malt syrup, and the salt) for about three minutes on low to medium speed. Once the batter has rested for twenty minutes, proceed (mixture autolysis). Now, add the salt and mix the mixture for a further four minutes on the lowest speed of your mixer. After four minutes, add the 6 ounces of water and the malt syrup gradually and combine again briefly.
- Drop the batter into a large monster-covered container and let the mixture rest at zone temperature until it is ready to use. Break up the assortment into halves using a gauge the next morning. Since the batter is sticky and moist, you'll need a bowl or plate to weigh it in. Each item ought to weigh no more than 1 pound, 14 ounces. Malt syrup gives the batter a sticky texture. With the measured batter still within the measuring bowl or plate, begin to draw up the edges and sides to form a ball. To reach the ball's inside, pull from its outside and squeeze.
- The consistency of the mixture is very sticky and sticky. Assemble certain the sealing material is very much dusted with semolina flour, and then lawfully shape the wet bundle of the variety into a ball before thwacking it into the container's center where the texture lining meets the sides. Quickly dust the remaining batter ball with semolina flour so it can't unwind and touch the texture around the edges. Combination for two hours at the zone temperature to confirm. For best results, preheat your oven to 450F/232C degrees while the batter has been curing for 60 minutes. Also, don't forget to heat up your simmering lies.

Soured Bread With Asiago From Kalamata

Cooking Time: 40 Minutes
Servings: 2
Nutritional Analysis:

Calories: 153

Total Fat: 3.88 g

Carbohydrates: 28.79 g

Fiber: 1.8 g

Ingredients:

- One pound, 6.5 ounces (637.9 grams) of bread flour, divided into five cups
- Three teaspoons of salt (about.6 ounces/17 g)
- Put in the following ingredients while rolling out the dough:
- Calamata Olives, 12 oz. (340 g)
- (8 oz. / 226 g) Asiago Cheese
- Culture for making white sourdough
- 5 ounces/141 grams of rye starter at 100% hydration
- 1/4 cup liquid = 4 oz (113 g)
- milk, evaporated, 1/2 cup (four ounces/113 grams)
- Oil: 2 tablespoons (1 ounce/28 grams)
- One ounce (about 28 grams) of fresh, chopped rosemary

Instructions:

- First thing in the morning, using your combination Mixer, mix together all of the ingredients in the great list except the salt. Approximately two to three minutes should be all that is needed. Twenty minutes of autolysis of the mixture.
- Then, for about five minutes, combine at moderate speed after adding salt. Since it is a one-day batter and won't go through as a few hours building up the gluten, the consolidation for Its combination is longer than for a typical sourdough. The batter should be flipped out into a collapsible box or container after the combining process is complete.
- Allow the batter to rest for six hours, then stir it every 60 minutes. As the mixture collapses, you'll notice that it becomes steadier. After letting the batter rest for six hours, divide it into two halves, each of which should weigh about one pound and eleven ounces (765 grams). For best results, let the ingredients 5-10 minutes to settle. It was planned that the quantities would be formed 30 minutes apart, so that they wouldn't be sealed at the same time. Then, pass the cheese, olives, and fresh Rosemary around. Cut the Rosemary leaves in half, 3D-square the cheddar, and channel the olives.

Sourdough Made With Cracked Wheat Flour

Cooking Time: 20 Minutes
Servings: 3
Nutritional Analysis:

Calories: 153

Total Fat: 3.28 g

Carbohydrates: 28.89 g

Fiber: 2.1 g

Ingredients:

- One pound, eight ounces of cracked wheat is equivalent to one-third of a cup.
- One pound of bread flour (about six and a quarter cups' worth) 1,43 Grams
- An ounce and a half of salt is equal to four teaspoons.
- Use a sourdough starter and make two cups of bread.
- 14 ounces of room temperature water, or one cup.
- Oil: 2 tbsp = 1 oz.

Instructions:

- Mix all the ingredients (except the salt) on a medium speed until well combined. It usually just takes a few minutes to do. Then, let the combination autolyze (rest) for twenty minutes per the license.
- Add salt after autolysis, then consolidate at low speed for about a further second. At this time, wait 7-8 hours, or until the mixed mass has matured (which signifies the primary ascent). To produce and align the gluten strands, the batter should be layered and massaged many times. If you want to age your combination in the Mixer, you should press the start button and let the snare rotate the bowl around twice while on the lowest natural setting. If you're using a batter collapsing holder, flip the mixture over every half an hour or so and cover it. Once the dough has matured, turn it out onto a lightly floured surface and knead it two or three times before shaping it into a ball.
- Divide the mixture into two objects of about two pounds each. Form ingredients into the shape you require, and then let the batter rest for ten minutes (seat rest). Lined crates or containers (Bannetons don't need lining) should be filled to capacity with the conditioned quantities and sealed. Leave the mixture to cool for about 30 minutes, then cover it with plastic wrap and place it in the fridge. Allow the batter two or three hours of clear evidence in the morning (at whatever point the mixture looks around one-half times the primary size). The batter should then be turned out onto the strip. Prepare in a preheated oven of 450F/232C for 20 minutes after slicing, washing, and covering with a boiling lid. After 20 minutes, remove the lid from the pan, reduce the heat to 425 degrees Fahrenheit (218 degrees Celsius), and continue cooking for another 15 minutes, or until a bread thermometer inserted into the center registers 200 degrees Fahrenheit (93 degrees Celsius), turning once halfway through cooking for caramelization.
- Remove the required quantity and let to cool on a rack. If the first batch is too brown, reduce the broiler temperature to 400F/204C for the second heat instead of 425F/218C. To re-fit the following quantity, please return the cooking cover back on the burner and reheat to 450F/232C. That's right, we're talking about San Francisco. A sourdough loaf has a thick exterior, a chewy inside, and a ton of air pockets. Actually, it's very tasty!
  - Half a cup of evaporated canned milk (4.0 ounces), one tablespoon of Malt syrup (.8 ounces)

Northwestern Sourdough

Cooking Time: 30 Minutes
Servings: 2
Nutritional Analysis:
Calories: 169
Total Fat: 3.28 g
Carbohydrates: 28.89 g
Fiber: 4.1 g

Ingredients:

- Exactly 34 ounces, or seven cups, of bread flour.
- half a cup of active sourdough starter, or 4.5 ounces
- Starter for the Northwest, one cup, 166% hydration, 9.0 ounces
- 12.0 ounces is equal to one and a half cups.
- 4.08 ounces of salt (add after dough autolysis)

Instructions:

- Mix all of the ingredients (except the salt) together for at least two minutes on low speed, preferably longer. The next step is to allow the mixture to autolyze (rest) for 20 minutes. Incorporate salt after autolysis, then consolidate the mixture for five minutes at a slow pace. Bread loaves created using a consolidate and heat method on a single day need additional joining time to develop their gluten structure. Allow the ingredients to mass develop (the crucial rise) for 4 hours.

- During the four-hour mass maturation, mix the mixture down by just three revolutions of the batter snare twice. Rather of weakening and collapsing the gluten strands, this process fortifies and aligns them. When you're ready to form a ball, dump the batter onto a surface dusted with flour (whole wheat flour) and knead it several times. Separate the batter into quarters.

- Form the batter into thick ropes of about 18 inches in length and let it sit for 5-10 minutes (seat rest). After the dough has rested, shape it into its final form by crisscrossing two pieces of the rope-shaped batter. Tightly encircle the winds with the hitter. To seal the containers or dish, place the quantities on the sealing materials that have been dusted with flour. Put one portion in the fridge or freezer for 40 minutes to halt the measuring process. To prevent the combination from drying out, either keep the sealing box moist or cover the portions with wet materials or plastic equipment. When you have an hour left to seal, heat the burner to 425F/218C and get out the stone and broiling cover.

- When the dough is ready and has a light, airy, and springy texture without being too sticky, remove a sufficient quantity by gently scooping it out of the banneton and placing it on a dusted strip. To use the new heating stone, cut the mixture together with the twists and put on the stone. Quickly drench the finished batter with water, and then cover with a hot lid. Please devote about twenty minutes for prepping. After 20 minutes have passed, turn the broiler heat down to 400F/204C and begin boiling the food on the stovetop. Ten minutes of continued heating, with most of the time spent in a sautéing position, is required. Remove the bread from the oven and place it on a cooling rack. Now, preheat the stove top for 5-10 minutes at 425 degrees Fahrenheit (218 degrees Celsius) before adding the next batch.

- Put the bread in the fridge and eat it with margarine all day. The first day after being baked, sourdough loaves taste the finest. If you sprinkle some on top with sesame or poppy seeds, the quantity becomes horrifyingly decent. Before cutting, brush the mixture with an egg wash made from one egg beaten with one Tablespoon of water. After slicing the egg-washed mixture, sprinkle the seeds on top. Get the necessary preparations underway.

Sourer Bread With Rosemary And Tubs

Cooking Time: 30 Minutes
Servings: 2
Nutritional Analysis:

Calories: 153

Total Fat: 3.8 g

Carbohydrates: 30.89 g

Fiber: 1.7 g

Ingredients:

- Two 9-ounce cups of bread flour
- 9 ounces (1 cup) of a healthy sourdough starter.
- 10 ounces, or one-fourth of a cup, of water.
- Rye Flour (0.5 Cups) / 1.8 Ounces

Instructions:

- Mix everything together (except the salt) until it's completely combined, then let the dough sit for 20 minutes (dough autolysis). Stir in the salt when the dough has finished autolyzing, and then work the dough for four minutes at a low pace.
- First, bulk ferment (or first rise) the dough for 4 to 6 hours, or until doubled in size. Every hour, give the dough a good folding or stirring. As soon as the dough has finished bulk fermentation, turn it out onto a lightly floured surface and knead just until it comes together in a ball.
- Cut the dough in half. Make a loaf in about the desired form, and then let it rest for 5-10 minutes (bench rest). Spread out the process of shaping the loaves by 30 minutes. Loaves should be proofed in bannetons for a half an hour to two hours, or until they have doubled in size.

Hercules, The Hercules Of Sour Dough

Cooking Time: 50 Minutes
Servings: 4
Nutritional Analysis:

Calories: 155

Total Fat: 3.7 g

Carbohydrates: 28 g

Fiber: 4.1 g

Ingredients:

- Two big eggs, about 3.50 ounces, beaten
- Two ounces of honey (equivalent to a quarter cup) and one and a half ounces of sugar
- Two Tablespoons of Vanilla Flavoring (.30 Ounce)
- Starter for sourdough bread, 1 cup
- Water: 4 ounces, or half a cup
- four ounces, or about half a cup, of canned milk
- four ounces of oil or melted butter, half a cup
- So, get out your Able skiver dish and start breeding some Able skivers. As an alternative to the usual pancakes or waffles, they make a delightful little snack.

Instructions:

- If you come across a good, sturdy metal Able skiver container, grab it. Mine is well-seasoned and well-worn. The surface rust on the base won't go away until I use a metal scrubber, which I won't do since it will return in a heartbeat in my climate. The player may be stocked with seven little disappointments.
- A drop of water should sizzle and jump when dropped into the container. Lubricate the little pots and pans. Next, have the player fill each downturn as you wait for the Able skiver to set almost nothing.
- Next, insert a thin, sharp blade or a perfect sewing needle into the hitter until it reaches the bottom of the little bowl. Using the rim, you spin the Able skiver up, and the central player falls out, starting the cooking process in the bowl's bottom third. An Able skiver produces a hollow ball by being turned continuously during cooking.

Sunrise Soubise

Cooking Time: 50 Minutes
Servings: 4
Nutritional Analysis:

Calories: 113

Total Fat: 6.28 g

Carbohydrates: 30.89 g

Fiber: 3.1 g

Ingredients:

- Rye flour, one and a half to three cups
- One and a half cups of whole wheat flour, or 1.4 ounces
- only one brewing process in progress
- 16 ounces, or two cups, of water.
- 3 cups (13.5 ounces) of bread flour

Instructions:

- Mix the ingredients together well, then set the bowl aside for 20 minutes to rest (batter autolysis). After the autolysis of the mixture, add the salt and mix the butter again briefly at a moderate speed.
- Hold off on checking the Its mixture until 6 o'clock at night. At that time, portion out the food and place it in plastic-lined containers or bowls before placing them in the cooler for the night. Take out the numbers on your own the next morning; good practice to wait at least 30 minutes between removals. The batter has to rest and prove for two to two and a half hours, or until the volume of the mixture has increased by about half.
- Now, cut the mixture while it's still on the strip, slide it into a fresh, warmed 450F/232.2C degree broiler onto a hot heating stone, quickly spritz the batter with water once, and cover with a cooking top that has already been preheated on the stove. To get ready, please allow twenty minutes.
- When the 20 minutes are up, lower the broiler temperature to 400F/204.4C and start the broiling cover. Keep cooking until a bread thermometer registers 200 205F/93 96C, which should take another 18 to 25 minutes. Toss the quantity about halfway during the final cooking time. Cool. Turn the stove copy and place the cooking cover back in to warm for 5 to 10 minutes, or until the supplementary quantity is ready to put in.

Chapter 12: Sweet Bread Recipes
Souring' With Butter And Honey

Cooking Time: 40 Minutes
Servings: 2
Nutritional Analysis:

Calories: 150

Total Fat: 4.28 g

Carbohydrates: 45.89 g

Fiber: 5.1 g

Ingredients:

- 4 ounces (113 grams) of softened butter, at room temperature
- There are three big eggs (beaten slightly before putting in Mixer) Weight: 5.2 oz. (147 g)
- Honey or malt syrup, 1/4 cup (3 ounces; 85 grams)
- 27 ounces (765 grams) of sourdough starter (3 cups at 166% hydration).
- 8 ounces (226 grams) of evaporated milk (or half-and-half milk) equals one cup.

Instructions:

- Put these components together as tightly as possible. Put the ingredients for the mixture in a separate bowl. Stir the dry ingredients together with a spoon until they are completely combined, and then add them to the wet ingredients in the Mixer. Get out the mixer and give it a good whirl, mixing for as long as you can to ensure that all ingredients are included.
- Empty the cornbread batter into a large, greased Bundt pan or cake dish that holds seventeen cups. Up to three quarters of the skillet's sides will be returned by the player. To give the cornmeal time to absorb the liquid, I let the player sit for an hour. I prepared the broiler to 400 degrees Fahrenheit (204 degrees Celsius), placed the bread in a sealed container, and sautéed it for fifty minutes.
- Its recipe yields a whopping 4 lb. 4 oz of cornbread, but you can easily halve the quantities for a more manageable Bundt cake.

Sour Bread Made With Lentils And Wheat Flour

Cooking Time: 30 Minutes
Servings: 2
Nutritional Analysis:

Calories: 166

Total Fat: 3.5 g

Carbohydrates: 28.30 g

Fiber: 1.1 g

Ingredients:

- Combine the lentils with a hand blender until they resemble flour. So, we're going to need some water and spelt flour.
- Put the concoction in a sealed container.
- half a cup (100 ml) dry green lentil
- One hundred milliliters (50 ml) of room temperature water
- a tablespoon of sifted all-purpose flour
- 100 milliliters (50 ml) of room temperature water

Instructions:

- Put in the water. Stir together and store in a glass container for two to four days. Blend in the early and late hours of the day. When the mixture begins to bubble, it's time to make the starter. Feeding the dough from then on will keep its taste and fermentation potential intact.
- To maintain the sourdough in the fridge, you need to feed it once a week with half a cup (one hundred milliliters) of water and one cup (one hundred grams) of lentil flour, which is roughly? cup (one hundred and fifty milliliters). The sourdough starter has to be fed the same amount of flour and water each day if it is to be kept at room temperature. You want it to have the consistency of thick porridge. You'll use one-cup freezer bags for any remaining sourdough.

Freshly Baked Whole-Wheat Houston Sourdough

Cooking Time: 30 Minutes
Servings: 2
Nutritional Analysis:

Calories: 166

Total Fat: 3.5 g

Carbohydrates: 28.30 g

Fiber: 1.1 g

Ingredients:

- There are 22 cups (1114 ounces) of water in this recipe.
- Two cups of sourdough flour, measured and
- a single teaspoon of kosher salt
- spoonful of olive oil
- Sourdough starter, 4 ounces
- rye flour; 1 cup (about 4 12 ounces)
- Spray oil for baking that isn't currently in stock

Instructions:

- Mix the sourdough starter with the remaining three-quarters of a cup of water, the sourdough flour, salt, and olive oil in a bowl. Combine using the batter snare of a Stand Mixer or by hand until uniform. Don't be tempted to add more flour since the batter is sticky and moist. Prepare a 9-by-5-inch size dish with a quick sprinkle of water and transfer the mixture to the pan.
- Spread the mixture evenly in the container using lightly lubricated hands. Wrap the dish in plastic wrap or put the whole pan inside a very large plastic bag. The sourdough may be refrigerated for as little as one hour or as long as 24 hours before use.

Hoochy Mamma Sourdough

Cooking Time: 30 Minutes
Servings: 2
Nutritional Analysis:

Calories: 130

Total Fat: 3.5 g

Carbohydrates: 28 g

Fiber: 1.5 g

Ingredients:

- Amount of sugar equal to one tablespoon
- 1/4 teaspoon of salt (preferably kosher)
- olive oil, 1 tsp.
- 3/4 cup of water at room temperature
- 2 1/4 teaspoons of dried active yeast
- 1 pound (three cups) of sourdough starter
- flour, and then some
- Gluten-free flour made from rice (for dusting the loaves)

Instructions:

- Combine everything save the oil and rice flour in a large bowl, then turn it upside down and work the mixture with your hands until it is well combined and less shaggy, or use a stand mixer with a batter hook to do the job quickly. You would want it not to become malleable. Whatever the case may be, it must be quite constrained and perceptive. Olive oil should be sprinkled into a gallon-sized, zero-inch-high plastic bag, and the mixture should then be transferred to the sack. (First, flour your hands, since the mixture will be sticky.)
- Roll the batter inside the package to coat it with olive oil. The oil will be redistributed throughout the mixture and the plastic bag with only a quick back massage, despite the sticky texture. Remove the air, reseal, and store in the fridge, at least temporarily. As the mixture matures in the fridge, feel free to do so the day before.

Soured Wheat And Molasses

Cooking Time: 50 Minutes
Servings: 4
Nutritional Analysis:

Calories: 173

Total Fat: 3.29 g

Carbohydrates: 35.89 g

Fiber: 2.1 g

Ingredients:

- 2 tbsp of black molasses
- Wheat bran, one and a quarter cup (34 grams) with two ounces (56.7 grams) of
- Bread flour, 11.1 ounces (286 grams) for 2 1/4 cups
- Measurement in Ounces: 595 grams/21 Ounces Whole Wheat Flour
- a potent starting in the amount of 1.5 cups
- Water Capacity for One Cup: 8 Ounces
- One and a half to two cups of coffee, strong and served at room temperature (around 6 ounces/ 170 grams)
- oil equivalent to two tablespoons
- three-quarters of a teaspoon

Instructions:

- It will take you around two to three minutes to combine the ingredients while mixing on medium speed. Allow the batter to autolyze (rest) for 20 minutes at this stage. After autolysis, include the other ingredients and blend for around two minutes on low speed. Leave the batter to rise for four to six hours until it has doubled in size. After the dough has had time to rise, turn it out onto a surface lightly dusted with flour (we use wheat flour) and knead it several times before rolling it into a ball. The batter should be separated into two huge chunks.

- Make measurements in a rough outline of what you desire, and then let the batter rest for five minutes (seat rest). After the quantities have been sorted, they are formed into their final forms and placed in the sealing crates or dish lined with sealing materials (bannetons are not need to be lined). Put in the fridge for now. The next morning, after allowing the mixture to boil and confirm, you may discard the batter staggered at forty-minute intervals. Taking the main portion, sprinkle the top (really the base) with semolina or whole grain flour, and pour the batter out onto a strip of flat heating sheet when the mixture is organized and feels effervescent and springy but not drooping.

- Then, while the batter is still on the strip, break it into pieces and slip it into a prepared broiler set to 450F/232.2C. Place a hot heating stone on top of the batter, quickly sprinkle it with water once, and cover with a boiling top.

- Twenty minutes of heating time is recommended. After 20 minutes, remove the lid from the pan and reduce the heat to 400F/204.4C. Cook for a another 18–25 minutes, or until a bread thermometer registers 200 F (205C). Approximately halfway through the final preparation sum for cooking, turn the quantity. Cool. In order to get the additional quantity ready to go in, you need invert the broiler, save a second copy, and put the simmering top back in the oven for 5 to 10 minutes. Relax and enjoy being doused in the ever-expanding spread while you chill out. Toasting this bread is a delight.

Sour Dough From San Francisco

Cooking Time: 30 Minutes
Servings: 2
Nutritional Analysis:

Calories: 153

Total Fat: 3.9 g

Carbohydrates: 28 g

Fiber: 5.1 g

Ingredients:

- One and a half cups (3 ounces) semolina flour One teaspoon (0.5 g) kosher salt
- spoonful of olive oil
- Water, about a quarter cup, at room temperature
- 2 1/4 teaspoons of dried active yeast
- Amount of sugar equal to one tablespoon
- Bread starter; 21.2 cups (1114 ounces) sourdough
- one and a half cups of pumpkin seeds,
- Spray oil for baking that isn't currently in stock

Instructions:

- Ply by hand (combine first in a huge basin, then flip out and massage) or in an exceptionally stand Mixer equipped with the batter snare until the mixture is pliable; the egg wash may be added at the end. After the mixture has been stirred, cover the bowl with plastic wrap and place it in a warm area for about an hour, or until the mixture has doubled in size. While waiting, fill a smaller-than-usual pan (534 inches by 3 inches) with hot shower water.
- After inverting the batter, spread it out on a floured surface and divide it into four equal halves. Using your own two hands, flatten the batter into a rough five-inch square. Then, using a jellyroll technique, roll the batter into a thick log. Squeeze the crease and end to seal, and then lay the record, crease side down, into one of the prepared dishes.
- Continue with the last three components of the blend. Wrap the dish in plastic wrap or place the items on a heating sheet (for easier maintenance), then place the whole container inside a large plastic bag and secure the opening. Put in the fridge for at least an hour, and up to 24, then cook when ready.

Sourdough With Nuts That Is Free Of Gluten

Cooking Time: 30 Minutes
Servings: 2
Nutritional Analysis:

Calories: 163

Total Fat: 3.28 g

Carbohydrates: 28.89 g

Fiber: 3.1 g

Ingredients:

- 1/4 teaspoon of salt (preferably kosher)
- 14 cups of cornstarch
- Xanthan gum, one tablespoon
- chopped walnuts equaling a quarter cup
- one-fourth cup of the seeds from a sunflower
- 14 cup of ground flax seeds
- Spray oil for cooking that is not in stock
- A total of 212 cups (or 1334 ounces) King
- Gluten-free King Arthur Flour
- general-purpose flour
- Count: 3
- cups, at room temperature, two
- cup and a half of fat-free powdered milk
- 2 1/4 teaspoons of dried active yeast
- a quarter of a cup of sesame seeds +
- added to the sourdough's crust
- a tablespoon of unsalted butter,

Instructions:

- Sprinkle some cooking splash (not preparation splash, which includes flour) onto a nine by five-inch quantity dish. You might also use oil to coat the pan if you like. Put all of the ingredients into a Stand mixer that has an oar connector.
- You're going to sign on, too. It's a huge bowl equipped with a hand mixer. For five minutes, beat. Although the top won't look like sourdough batter, the mixture will start to look almost non-sticky, like overcooked mashed potatoes.
- Place the batter in the prepared pan and spread it out with wet fingertips. Wrap the skillet with plastic wrap or place it inside a large plastic bag and secure the opening. Keep the batter chilled for at least 4 hours and up to 24 hours.

Sourdough Made With Seasoned Yeast Wood

Cooking Time: 20 Minutes
Servings: 3
Nutritional Analysis:

Calories: 153

Total Fat: 3.58 g

Carbohydrates: 30 g

Fiber: 3.1 g

Ingredients:

- 6.75 ounces (1.25 cups) of Bread Flour
- Two and a half tablespoons of whole wheat or spelt flour.
- 1 oz.
- Strong sourdough starter, 1 cup
- A standard cup of water contains eight fluid ounces.
- Rye Flour, 14 Cup -

Instructions:

- Blend in the seasonings and salt for three minutes. Once that time has passed, the combination should age for another four hours at the very least. When the dough is ready, turn it out onto a lightly floured area and knead it until it comes together in a ball. Separate the mixture into halves. Form the dough into your desired form, and then let it rest for 5-10 minutes (seat rest).
- Once you've completed the sidelining process, you may shape the quantities into their final bodies and place them in the lined bannetons or sealing containers. For the time being, place bushels in a plastic bag and chill them in the refrigerator. Take readings at 30-minute intervals first thing in the morning, then let the batter rest and rise for a couple of hours. Then, broil at 450F/232C until the top is golden brown, cut it, splash it once, and cover it. Get ready to wait 20 minutes.
- Leave the stovetop, taking careful of the fresh steam, after the timer goes off. Then, after 15–20 minutes further of cooking at 425F/218C with the oven door ajar, the bread should reach an internal temperature of 200–205F/93–96C on a bread thermometer. Cool. Take in enough of margarine when you eat.

Traditional Sourdine Bread

Cooking Time: 30 Minutes
Servings: 2
Nutritional Analysis:

Calories: 190

Total Fat: 6.28 g

Carbohydrates: 30 g

Fiber: 3.1 g

Ingredients:

- 3 Cups a cup of whole wheat flour or all-purpose flour
- honey for the malt in a recipe calling for a half cup of all-purpose flour
- syrup, you may make Honey Whole Wheat Pancakes. - 1.32 Pounds (374 Grams)
- half an ounce (14 grams) of baking powder (one table spoon)
- a half cup of melted butter that has been refrigerated
- Evaporated milk, 8 ounces (226 grams) per cup
- 1 / 2 cup of water equals 4 ounces (113 grams).
- Using a strong sourdough starter, mix 2 cups
- You'll need one ounce (or 28 grams) of malt syrup or honey to make one hearty serving.
- Baking soda, 1 teaspoonful (.16 oz./4.5 g)
- Measurements for salt in teaspoons:.2 ounces (5.7 g)

Instructions:

- Add the dry ingredients to the wet ones now, and stir gently. Make sure your iron is nice and hot, at 375F/190C degrees, and let the player rest for about ten to fifteen minutes so the flour can absorb the moisture. Lightly grease the pan. You want one side of your hotcakes to be bubbly and the edges to be just a little bit dry after you're done ironing them. Turn the frying pan to the other side and give it a quick turn.
- Sending a new margarine and some maple syrup as a gift (we will, in general, add Malt syrup to our Maple syrup for extra flavor). We expected to get many requests, so we prepared to field many questions on persuasion. The recipe yields twenty pancakes, plenty for a large family or many more servings. Therefore, divide the totals in half for a more reasonable class.

Chapter 13: Gluten Free Bread Recipes
Sourdough Bread, White, Whole Wheat

Cooking Time: 50 Minutes
Servings: 4
Nutritional Analysis:

Calories: 158

Total Fat: 5 g

Carbohydrates: 29 g

Fiber: 3.5 g

Ingredients:

- Sourdough flour, 2 cups
- 1.2 ounces (3.5 grams) of dark rye flour
- 1-2 teaspoons of kosher salt
- Vital wheat gluten, 1 tsp.
- Two tablespoons of sugar
- three quarters of a cup plus a tablespoon of water, preferably at room temperature
- A teaspoon of dried active yeast
- A Single Teaspoon of Sugar
- a quarter cup of wheat flour (around 338 ounces)
- a pinch or two of kosher salt
- Unsalted butter, one teaspoon

Instructions:

- The instructions for all three batters are the same: Put all the ingredients into a medium bowl or the bowl of your stand mixer and mix until combined. From there, you can either massage the mixture by hand or use the mixture snare attachment on your mixer to make it more malleable. The rye batter, then the wheat and white flour, is what I recommend making first. (Since rye grows a little slower than wheat, you may give it a head start; white grows the quickest.) When all of the batter has been prepared, put it in a medium bowl, cover it, and set it aside in a warm location.
- When you're ready to let the batter rise for the third and final Mixture, set a timer for 45 minutes. Use insulating paper to line a heating pad. After the batters have risen, lightly dust your workspace with flour. Then, one by one, take each Mixture and shape it into a rope (much how a child might roll a snake out of soil), with a total length of about 20 inches. Arrange the three Mixture pieces in close proximity to one another. Gather the three into a tight ball and push it to one side. When you reach that stage, you may freely interlace them.
- When you're done, be sure to firmly close the lids. The batter should be transferred to the sheet coated with the material. If I need extra room on the sheet, I will arrange it crookedly. Tuck the compressed edges underneath to hide them, then plan and adjust the batter until it's uniform. Wrap tightly with plastic wrap and store in the fridge for at least a few hours and up to 24.

Two Tablespoons' Garlic Onion Sourdough One Ounce Oil

Cooking Time: 30 Minutes

Servings: 4

Nutritional Analysis:

Calories: 105

Total Fat: 4 g

Carbohydrates: 28 g

Fiber: 1.5 g

Ingredients:

- 0.7 grams (one teaspoon) of cracked black pepper
- Dill Seeds (one Tablespoon) =.23 Grams
- A Single Cup, Please
- Equal to One Cup of Molasses
- A Single Particle of Granulated Onion
- One serving (8 ounces) of evaporated milk yields one cup.
- .08 oz (1 tablespoon) of flaked red pepper

Instructions:

- Mix in 4 tablespoons of salt and 5 1/4 cups of bread flour. Stir the ingredients, salt included, for eight osmics on medium speed until combined. It should just take two or three minutes. It's going to be a sticky mixture. Once the combination has rested (autolyzed) for 20 minutes, you may proceed. Follow the autolysis with about four minutes of slow-speed mixing in a mixer. Then, wait about four hours for the bulk of the combination to grow and multiply. Afterwards, dump the blended ingredients onto a lightly floured (Rye flour) surface and ply it a few times. It eventually rolls up into a ball. Cut the batter in half so that you have two huge halves. Amounts should be arranged in the desired pattern, and the Mixture should be left to sit for 10 minutes (seat rest).

- To maintain a moist Mixture, cover the quantities with textiles and sprinkle water over them gently, or place the batter, bannetons, and each into separate plastic bags. Let the mixture sit for an hour to three hours, or until ready. Rye bread can often ruin if over proofed. Turn the temperature up to 450 degrees Fahrenheit (232.2 degrees Celsius) on the stove. After the batter has set and feels bubbly and springy but not droopy, dust the top (actually the underside) with semolina or whole-grain flour and turn it out onto a strip of flat baking sheet. When you're ready to cook, pour the batter out onto a long strip. Then, cut the batter while it's still on the strip, place it on a hot, warmed baking stone in an oven set to 450F/232.2C, quickly sprinkle the Mixture with water, and cover it with a boiling lid. Plan on spending the next twenty minutes getting ready.

- When the 20 minutes are up, lower the heat to 400 degrees Fahrenheit (204.4 degrees Celsius) and cover the pot to keep it at a simmer. Using a bread thermometer, ensure the bread reaches an internal temperature of 200 205F/93 96C by continuing to bake it for an additional 18–25 minutes. For a more even sear, flip the quantity halfway through the final cooking total. Cool. Next, warm the broiler for five to ten minutes, or until the quantity is ready to go in, by turning it on, making a copy, and placing the cooking cover back in its original place. Melt the same amount as the real thing. Cool It's great with a fresh condiment or some cream cheese. Bread has a subtle, made-from-scratch garlicky, onion taste; it's great for meat sandwiches from the deli case.

Salty Modern Sourdough

Cooking Time: 40 Minutes
Servings: 1
Nutritional Analysis:

Calories: 180

Total Fat: 5 g

Carbohydrates: 30 g

Fiber: 1.81 g

Ingredients:

- half a cup of rye flour
- Eight and a half cups of Bread Flour
- Austrian sourdough starter, two cups
- One and a half cups, or 12 ounces, is the equivalent of one cup.
- Six ounces of evaporated milk make up one-third of a cup.
- Amount of Salt: 4.5 tsp

Instructions:

- Mix all ingredients (except salt) together until uniform, then set aside for 20 minutes to rest (batter autolysis). After the batter has undergone autolysis, added the salt and mixed it in on a low speed for a few minutes. Then, after the initial ascent, let the combination sit for six hours to massage. During the six-hour massage process, place the Mixture in a collapsible box and fold it once per hour.
- After the batter has had enough time to ferment, it should be poured onto a lightly floured surface and worked with until it forms a ball. Split the batter in half and set each half aside. Form each portion into the final form, and then place them in the storage containers, dish, or Couche to rest for five to ten minutes (seat rest) once you've finished shaping the batter.
- Plastic bags may be used to cover the batter and chill it until you're ready to use it. Allow the batter to definite evidence for two to three hours (when the mixture looks about half its size and is elastic/springy), then turn it out on a strip and slice it, then shower it, cover it with a simmering lid, and cook it in a preheated 425F/218C oven for 20 minutes. After 20 minutes, take the lid off the pot and reduce the heat to 400F/204C. Continue cooking for another 10 to 15 minutes, rotating often to get a caramelized crust.
- At 200-205 degrees Fahrenheit (93-96 degrees Celsius), the inside of the bread is done. Remove a serving and let it to cool on a rack. Keep the stove at 425F/218C degrees during the whole heating duration on the following plan if the base quantity seems too earthy colored. Be sure to warm the broiler cover before inserting the resultant quantity inside.

Delish Sourdough Made With Whole-Wheat Flour

Cooking Time: 35 Minutes
Servings: 2
Nutritional Analysis:

Calories: 125

Total Fat: 3 g

Carbohydrates: 28 g

Fiber: 3 g

Ingredients:

- How many ounces of whole wheat flour are in a cup?
- There are 9 ounces in a cup of sourdough starter at 166% hydration.
- 16 ounces, or two cups, of water.
- Buckwheat: one cup (or 4.6 ounces) of roughly milled
- Fourteen ounces of bread flour is equivalent to two cups.

Instructions:

- Mix the ingredients together until uniform, except the salt (concerning a couple of – three minutes). After that, let the batter 20 minutes to chill (mixture autolysis). As the mixture autolyzes, add the salt and continue consolidating the batter on low speed for another four minutes. Let the batter rest for at least four hours, or until it has doubled in size. After that, form the quantities, with each form being 30 minutes apart.
- The combination has to heat and confirm for about two to two and a half hours, or until the volume increases by about half.
- In a fresh, prepared oven at 450 degrees Fahrenheit (232.2 degrees Celsius), place the batter strips on a hot heating stone, quickly sprinkle the mixture with water, and cover with a boiling top. Get ready for the next 20 minutes.
- After 20 minutes, fire up the stove and reduce the temperature of the broiler to 400F/204.4C. If your bread thermometer reads 93-96 degrees Celsius, bake for another 18-25 minutes. To sear the meat, flip the quantity halfway through the final cooking total. Cool. When you're ready to cook the resulting quantity, return the burner to a simmering setting at 450F/232.2C.

Waterfront Farm Soubise

Cooking Time: 40 Minutes
Servings: 3
Nutritional Analysis:

Calories: 153

Total Fat: 3.6 g

Carbohydrates: 28 g

Fiber: 1.8 g

Ingredients:

- Two Tablespoons of melted, cooled butter equals one Ounce.
- The weight in ounces of 4.2 ounces of whole wheat flour in a cup of this flour.
- Six and a quarter cups of bread flour (or around 28.1 ounces)
- Sourdough starter, two cups
- 10 ounces, or one-fourth of a cup, of water.
- The equivalent of 4 ounces of scalded and cooled half a cup of cream or half-and-half milk
- Salt, to taste: 0.4 tsp (.8 oz)

Instructions:

- Mix all ingredients except the salt together until incorporated, then let the mixture sit for 20 minutes (batter autolysis). At the end of the autolysis period, add the salt and mix the batter for about two minutes on a low speed. The batter mass has to rest (first rise) for at least six hours, preferably until it has multiplied. Place the Mixture in a collapsible container and cover it with a sheet of paper once per hour while massaging.
- The batter should be poured onto a lightly floured board and worked with until a ball can be formed. Splice the Blend in Half. Form the components into the desired form, then let the mixture 5 to 10 minutes to rest (seat rest). After being set aside, the figures' final bodies are tallied and placed in a sealed container, dish, or Couche.
- Wrap the Mixture in plastic and store it in the fridge for now. Early in the morning, once the mixture has doubled in size and is elastic, let it rest for another couple of hours. Next, spread the Mixture on a strip and slice pan, rinse it off, cover it with a cooking top, and broil it at a high temperature of 425F/218C for 20 minutes.
- After twenty minutes, take it off the heat so it's just simmering, turn the broiler down to 400F/204C, and keep it there for another ten to fifteen minutes, turning it over halfway through. You should remove the specified quantity and allow it to cool on a rack. If the first batch you make is too brown, you may avoid this by keeping the burner at 400F/204C degrees for the whole of the cooking time. Before you set up the following quantity, warm the broiling cover by placing it in the oven.

Sourdough Ciabatta

Cooking Time: 35 Minutes
Servings: 1
Nutritional Analysis:
Calories: 150
Total Fat: 5 g
Carbohydrates: 28 g
Fiber: 1.9g

Ingredients:

- a Single Measured Tablespoon of Oil (.5 Ounce)
- After dough autolysis, 2.5 tsp of salt is added (.5 Ounce)
- 18 ounces of our powerful 166% beginning
- 6 ounces of H2O
- Three-ounce cans of milk
- flour for baking bread, weighing 1 lb. 6 oz.

Instructions:

- The finished Mixture will have a 70% hydration level and may be made in two 1-pound, 9-ounce batches. Mix together all ingredients (except salt) for about three minutes on low to medium speed. The batter should rest for 20 minutes after this (autolysis).

- After adding the salt, mix the batter on low for an additional five minutes. In a collapsible box, place the batter and allow the Mixture sit for four hours at room temperature to develop. When the timer goes off, blend the batter or fold it in on itself. When the batter has been well worked, transfer it to a container with extra lining and store it in the fridge for the time being. The next morning, you have the option of letting the Mixture warm up in a sealed box (dishwasher) for an hour at roughly eighty-90F/26 32C degrees, or leaving it out in space for two hours. When the batter is ready to be used, pour it onto a surface that has been liberally dusted with flour. In terms of thickness, its Mixture is a star.

- One pound eight ounces of batter each serving, poured out onto a heavily floured surface to form a sticky protuberance. In its final form, the batter will seem like a lumpy mound on the flour. Now, fold the Mixture in half height wise, keeping your hands only on the floured sections of the batter. As time passes, it will harden up about averagely. Since you don't want to add too much flour to the wet ingredients, there's no need to work the batter. Keep a lot of flour around the edge of the mixture to prevent it from sticking. Remove it along with your half-baked scrubber if it sticks.

- Put the mixture in small amounts onto a floured heating sheet or a heavily floured Couche. After molding each portion, wait an hour to an hour and a half before checking the results. If the measurements are a little off, you may smooth them out by making dimples in the batter with your hands and pressing them into the Mixture. Spread the batter out as thin as possible before putting it under the broiler. Prepare in a preheated oven at 450F/232C for 15 minutes, then reduce heat to 425F/218C for another 15-18 minutes, or until a deep beautiful earthy red. Assuming your container is flat and has no sides, you may simply place the heating sheet directly onto the preparation stone, or slide the portions directly from the skillet onto the stone.

- If using a Couche, quantities should be printed onto a floured strip and then placed onto the hot stone in the new broiler. Covering the Mixture with a simmering lid for the required 12 minutes may provide far better results. Don't dampen the totals with a dash of water. Let the batter's steam try to do the job for you. Put the margarine on heavy and let the portions cool before serving.

Hearth Flaxseed Sourdough

Cooking Time: 45 Minutes
Servings: 3
Nutritional Analysis:

Calories: 179

Total Fat: 5g

Carbohydrates: 28 g

Fiber: 1.9 g

Ingredients:

- Rye Flour (for two to three cups): 2.4 ounces
- Use 12.6 ounces of whole wheat flour (3 cups).
- half a cup of all-purpose flour one pound and three and a half ounces of bread flour
- 18 ounces (2 cups) of active sourdough starter
- A 16-ounce bottle of hot water, enough for two cups.
- An ounce of oil is equal to two tablespoons.
- two TBSP malt syrup – one.6 Ounce
- 1/4 cup cornmeal = 1.2 ounces
- 4 teaspoons of salt (add salt after dough autolysis)

Instructions:

- Combine ingredients in a mixer on low to medium speed for about two minutes, or until smooth. Twenty minutes later, Dough had turned to autolysis. The next step is a six-hour massage in zero gravity. You may use a batter collapsing box (see Dough Folding) to fold the mass over once at regular intervals as it rises, or you can just leave the mixture in the mixer. You can save energy by just using three revolutions of the snare if you keep the mix in the mixer, switch it on low once an hour, and stir the batter.
- If you have been keeping your Mixture in the Mixer, add the seeds and wheat and combine them thoroughly into the batter, either by hand or at low speed. Drop batter onto a lightly floured surface, knead occasionally (just enough to form a ball), and divide in half. After shaping the batter into its final form, let it a rest for five to ten minutes. Finally, shape the quantities one final time and place them in bannetons or receptacles that have been sealed using the appropriate material and dusted with rye flour. Throw a plastic bag over the whole package. Put in the fridge for now. Time your morning eliminations so that your quantities have forty minutes to warm up before you seal and organize them for cooking (one. Five - three hours).
- To evenly distribute Flax seeds throughout the top of the exterior, whisk one egg with one Tablespoon of water, then brush the egg mixture over the dough before sprinkling with the seeds. Fractional Mixture. Drop the mixture onto a hot heating stone on a burner warmed to 425F/218C. Moving along quickly. The batter is covered with a broiling cover that has already been prepared in the broiler and sprayed with water. Please devote about twenty minutes for prepping. Once you reach that temperature, lower the heat to 400F/204C and start the cooking cover.
- Prepare for another 20–25 minutes, flipping the quantity once while cooking. A quick thermometer reading of 200 205F/93-96C is ideal for the bread. Bring the temperature up to 425F/218C and place the simmering cover back on the pot to warm until the following quantity is ready to be added. Substantial heat in proportion to requirements. Relax and enjoy the fresh spread you just put on. The toast and sandwiches at It Bread are excellent.

Sour Rye Bread With Slight Onions

Cooking Time: 40 Minutes
Servings: 2
Nutritional Analysis:

Calories: 153

Total Fat: 3.5 g

Carbohydrates: 28 g

Fiber: 1.9 g

Ingredients:

- Dry onion flakes, 3 tablespoons
- Caraway seeds, 2 tablespoons (0.5 ounces)
- Half a teaspoon of dried onion
- To season, use three-and-a-half-tenths of a
- the equivalent of two cups of Rye flour
- This sourdough starter has two personalities.
- Half a cup of water (around 14 ounces)
- 2 Tablespoons of Oil
- Malt syrup, one tablespoon (about 0.8 ounces)
- Amount of Whole Wheat Flour Needed: 2 Cups (or 8.4 Ounces)
- (13.5 ounces) equal to three cups of bread flour.

Instructions:

- For two to three minutes, mix together all ingredients (excluding salt). Autolysis of the dough followed by salting.
- Keep mixing for a full minute so the salt is well mixed. Let it sit and ferment for four to five hours, or until it has doubled in size. After mixing, dump the dough onto a lightly dusted (Whole Wheat or Rye flour works best) surface and knead it into a ball for four or five turns. Cut in half and shape each half into a loaf. To prove bread, turn upside-down loaves into dishes or baskets lined with a proving cloth and sprinkle with Rye flour.
- Don a plastic bag and let it chill in the fridge overnight. Take out the loaves 40 minutes apart in the morning, cover, and let rise (a pair of - three hours or until prepared).

Cooking Time: 40 Minutes
Servings: 2
Nutritional Analysis:

Calories: 180

Total Fat: 3.52 g

Carbohydrates: 30 g

Fiber: 1.5 g

Ingredients:

- Rye flour: 3.6 ounces (102 grams) for one cup's worth.
- For reference,.2 ounces (5.7
- Spring Wheat Flour, Sifted, 3 Cups
- Just one cup of whole wheat starter
- water for two cups, or 16 ounces (453 grams).

Instructions:

- Spread the mixture out onto a surface lightly dusted with flour (rye or wheat) and knead it several times. A ball should be formed at that moment. Wait 10 minutes before finishing the shaping after resting the mixture. Seal the crate with the appropriate material (Bannetons are not need to be lined) and place the mixture inside. Place the plastic bag over the top of the Mixture container and store it in the refrigerator temporarily.
- Get rid of it in the morning and wait one to three hours to show your proof. When the batter is ready, you can tell because it will have a bubbly, springy, not drooping, texture if you touch it. Sprinkle the top (really the base) with semolina or whole grain flour, and then turn the mixture out onto a strip of flat heating sheet. Then, cut the mixture while it's still on the strip and place it on a stone in a preheated oven at 450 degrees Fahrenheit (232 degrees Celsius). Quickly sprinkle the batter with water before covering it with a boiling top. For 20 minutes, heat. After 20 minutes, turn down the broiler temperature to 400F/204C and begin the simmering cover.
- Sear the meat by continuing to cook it for another 40 minutes and flipping it over once. Check the internal temperature of the quantity using a bread thermometer to make sure it's done cooking; it should register 200-205F/93-96C.
- Micha is at its best when let to cool down to room temperature, since doing so enhances both its taste and its texture. Eat with a lot of cream cheese and continuing spread.

Crusty Pumpkin Sourdough With Ripened Pumpkin

Cooking Time: 40 Minutes

Servings: 2

Nutritional Analysis:

Calories: 180

Total Fat: 3.52 g

Carbohydrates: 30 g

Fiber: 1.5 g

Ingredients:

- It takes one ounce of oil to fill a tablespoon.
- An ounce of honey or malt syrup, measured by the tablespoonful
- Four and a half cups of flour (or 20.2 ounces) of bread flour (or all-purpose flour).
- 1 cup of a healthy, mature starter
- 12 ounces is equal to half a cup.
- 13.5 ounces (about three cups) of bread flour
- .7 ounces (31/2) salt (should be added after the dough has autolyzed)

Instructions:

- Gather all of the components and combine them. Put your mixer onto medium or low speed. Turn off the Mixer and let the ingredients autolyze (rest) for 20 minutes after they have been combined. After the batter has rested for a while (the "autolysis phase"), turn the mixer back to its slowest setting and add the.9 ounce of salt. In order to develop the gluten, let the mixture solidify at a slow pace for around four minutes.
- It's going to be a sticky mixture. Return the seedlings to the batter collapsing box, or a large storage container, and let them to develop for four hours, or until 11:30 a.m. Overlapping the batter roughly once per hour in the collapsing box helps strengthen the gluten.
- Four hours after resting, divide the batter in half. Then, either use a Couche or a surface that has been well floured to shape and spot the quantities into the sealing containers, which have been fastened with intensively floured sealing fabrics. Form the second sum thirty minutes after the real sum to truly shock the players. They will then be heated on a number of different instances. Authorization requires compelling proof that should take no more than two hours to gather. Broiler temperature should be set to 450 degrees Fahrenheit (232.2 degrees Celsius) when there is roughly an hour left before cooking time. As soon as the Mixture is well-organized and springs back when lightly pressed, remove a main portion and pour the batter out onto a narrow, flat baking sheet. Pumpkin seeds may be pressed into the top of the batter and the cake can be cut into slices.
- Slide the Mixture onto a hot, prepared heating stone in a broiler warmed to 450F/232.2C, quickly sprinkle it with water, and then cover with a boiling top. Please devote about twenty minutes for prepping. After twenty minutes, turn on the broiler and lower the temperature to 400F/204.4C and start the simmering stove. Continue cooking for another 15 to 20 minutes, turning the quantity once to sauté.
- Turn the stove on, replicate 450F/232.2C, and return the simmering cover to the preheating position for the following amount. Substantial heat in proportion to requirements. It's possible the sum is a fluffy, ethereal pumpkin color with crunchy fried seeds on the top. A fantastic Halloween buffet cost might be manufactured using this.

Conclusion

We hope you enjoyed our book about the Bread Machine Cookbook. We hope you'll find a recipe or two that will become one of your favorites in this cookbook. If you enjoy baking bread at home, you must check out the bread machine cookbook. It is packed with the most delicious recipes that you will ever need. No matter your skill level or how much time you want to spend in the kitchen, the recipes in this book will make the process easier. Additionally, the recipes in this book are so easy to follow, you will be able to apply them to make all types of breads.

It's important to have a good bread machine cookbook to create wonderful loaves of bread. This is something that any baker should consider having. If you are starting to bake bread but don't know where to start, this is a good place to start.

Bread machines are very easy to use and they produce lots of different types of bread that are just as delicious as they are simple. You can make many different types of bread with a bread machine during the week and then freeze the leftovers for a quick breakfast or dinner. Make sure to always use our bread machine recipe eBook to find the best bread machine recipe for your machine.

Good Luck!

Basic Conversion Charts

weight
(rounded to the nearest whole number)

IMPERIAL	METRIC
0.5 oz	14 g
1 oz	28 g
2 oz	58 g
3 oz	86 g
4 oz	114 g
5 oz	142 g
6 oz	170 g
7 oz	198 g
8 oz (1/2 lb)	226 g
9 oz	256 g
10 oz	284 g
11 oz	312 g
12 oz	340 g
13 oz	368 g
14 oz	396 g
15 oz	426 g
16 oz (1 lb)	454 g
24 oz (1 1/2 lb)	680 g

misc
(rounded to the closest equivalent)

IMPERIAL	
1 quart	4 cups (1 liter)
4 quarts	16 cups (4.5 liters)
6 quarts	24 cups (7 liters)
1 gallon	16 cups (4.5 liters)

volume
(rounded to the closest equivalent)

IMPERIAL	METRIC
1/8 tsp	0.5 mL
1/4 tsp	1 mL
1/2 tsp	2.5 mL
3/4 tsp	4 mL
1 tsp	5 mL
1 tbsp	15 mL
1 1/2 tbsp	25 mL
1/8 cup	30 mL
1/4 cup	60 mL
1/3 cup	80 mL
1/2 cup	120 mL
2/3 cup	160 mL
3/4 cup	180 mL
1 cup	240 mL

liquid
(rounded to the closest equivalent)

IMPERIAL	METRIC
0.5 oz	15 mL
1 oz	30 mL
2 oz	60 mL
3 oz	85 mL
4 oz	115 mL
5 oz	140 mL
6 oz	170 mL
7 oz	200 mL
8 oz	230 mL
9 oz	260 mL
10 oz	285 mL
11 oz	310 mL
12 oz	340 mL
13 oz	370 mL

temperature
(rounded to the closest equivalent)

IMPERIAL	METRIC
150°F	65°C
160 °F	70 °C
175 °F	80 °C
200 °F	95 °C
225 °F	110 °C
250 °F	120 °C
275 °F	135 °C
300 °F	150 °C
325 °F	160 °C
350 °F	175 °C
375 °F	190 °C
400 °F	205 °C
425 °F	220 °C
450 °F	230 °C
475 °F	245 °C
500 °F	260 °C

length
(rounded to the closest equivalent)

IMPERIAL	METRIC
1/8 inch	3 mm
1/4 inch	6 mm
1 inch	2.5 cm
1 1/4 inch	3 cm
2 inches	5 cm
6 inches	15 cm
8 inches	20 cm
9 inches	22.5 cm
10 inches	25 cm
11 inches	28 cm

Cooking Measurement Conversion Chart

QUICK ALTERNATIVES

1	tablespoon (tbsp)	3	teaspoons (tsp)
1/16	cup	1	tablespoon
1/8	cup	2	tablespoons
1/6	cup	2	tablespoons + 2 teaspoons
1/4	cup	4	tablespoons
1/3	cup	5	tablespoons + 1 teaspoon
3/8	cup	6	tablespoons
1/2	cup	8	tablespoons
2/3	cup	10	tablespoons + 2 teaspoons
3/4	cup	12	tablespoons
1	cup	48	teaspoons
1	cup	16	tablespoons
8	fluid ounces (fl oz)	1	cup
1	pint (pt)	2	cups
1	quart (qt)	2	pints
4	cups	1	quart
1	gallon (gal)	4	quarts
16	ounces (oz)	1	pound (lb)
1	milliliter (ml)	1	cubic centimeter (cc)
1	inch (in)	2.54	centimeters (cm)

CAPACITY (U.S to Metric)

1/5 teaspoon	1 milliliter
1 teaspoon	5 ml
1 tablespoon	15 ml
1 fluid oz	30 ml
1/5 cup	47 ml
1 cup	237 ml
2 cups (1 pint)	473 ml
4 cups (1 quart)	.95 liter
4 quarts (1 gal.)	3.8 liters

WEIGHT (U.S to Metric)

1	oz	28 grams
1	pound	454 grams

CAPACITY (Metric to U.S.)

1 milliliter	1/5	teaspoon
5 ml	1	teaspoon
15 ml	1	tablespoon
100 ml	3.4	fluid oz
240 ml	1	cup
	34	fluid oz
	4.2	cups
1 liter	2.1	pints
	1.06	quarts
	0.26	gallon

WEIGHT (Metric to U.S.)

1	gram	0.035 ounce
100	grams	3.5 ounces
500	grams	1.1 pounds
1	kilogram	2.205 pounds
		35 ounces

Printed in Great Britain
by Amazon

87777775R00072